Wednesday's Children

Kathryn Anne Michaels

The events depicted in this book are true. All names, locations, and similar entities have been changed. Time lines, sequences of events, and other aspects may have been compressed or modified for continuity.

ISBN-13: 978-0-9981355-6-4 (paperback)
ISBN-13: 978-0-9981355-7-1 (e-book)

Cover art: SelfPubBookCovers.com/ Daniela

Monkeypaw Press

Published by Monkeypaw Press, LLC Charleston, SC

Lovingly dedicated to all the nation's Child Protective Services social workers, those underpaid, overworked, unappreciated heroes of our culture

Contents

Monday's child is fair of face,
Tuesday's child is full of grace,
Wednesday's child is full of woe,
Thursday's child has far to go.
Friday's child is loving and giving,
Saturday's child must work for a living.
But the child that is born on the Sabbath Day
is bright and bonnie, good and gay.

A. E. Bray – *Traditions of Devonshire*

Prologue

Lines of sweat trickled down my soot-smeared face, blending with my tears. The North Carolina summer morning was already sweltering, and dressed in heavy denim, leather gloves, and hiking boots, I picked my way slowly through the ashes of what, only a few days before, had been my home.

Friends searched through the still-smoldering rubble with me, clad the same way I was in heavy gear to protect them from the lingering heat of the fire. We were trying to find something—anything—that might have survived the inferno as a remnant of my past. Letters, photographs, a lifetime of memorabilia, as well as climbing ropes, mountain rescue gear, a collection of geodes—even a kayak—had all turned to ugly powdery ash along with my clothing and furniture in what the local fire department called the hottest fire they had seen in over a decade.

A silver gleam in the charred rubble caught my eye, and with my glove I pushed aside the hot ashes to reveal the lens ring of what remained of my beloved Canon camera.

"Kate! Look at this! I found one of your geodes!" My friend Donna's voice was ecstatic as she lifted the beautiful purple crystal out of the ankle-deep ash. When she opened her gloved hand, she exposed the geode to the ninety-degree heat of the day. Immediately the crystal, still super-heated from the blaze, exploded into a pile of dust.

I took the dust and the camera ring, sat down on a boulder, and cried.

I had been out of town visiting family when, according to the police, some

1

rogue members of the Ku Klux Klan had crept into the moonlit yard of my little farmhouse and launched a Molotov cocktail through the window of my bedroom.

Their motive? Revenge.

But I'm getting ahead of myself...

Of Spanish Moss and Chiggers

"I need to see the doctor right away."

It was the winter of 1970, and the country's modern Emergency Medical Services system was still in its infancy. It had certainly not yet arrived in what was then a tiny coastal town in the marshes of South Carolina where I lived and worked as a nurse for a physician in private practice. Although rough-and-ready forms of ambulances had existed since the pre-Napoleonic era, modern "aid cars" staffed by EMTs and paramedics who could start IVs, suture wounds, administer medications, and keep a critically ill patient stable during hospital transport were just making their appearance. My rural patients, leery of these and any other "high-tech" medical innovations, often shunned modern care in favor of old-time remedies or simple self-reliance.

Home remedies were pretty much the norm among the rural folk in this somewhat isolated area of what is still known as the South Carolina Lowcountry, which stretches along the barrier islands and saltwater marshes roughly from Hilton Head to Myrtle Beach. Here, doctor visits were generally a last-ditch effort by the patients when everything else had failed.

Thus I was not particularly surprised when I looked up from my desk in the small general practice clinic where I was employed to find a gray-haired farmer in coveralls looking down at me, his face pale and beaded with sweat.

"I kinda nicked m' leg with the chainsaw," he said in that slow Lowcountry drawl that held a trace of what the locals called *Geechee*.

Familiar with the accent and the people who spoke it, I did a quick mental translation: *Kinda nicked m' leg* most likely meant a severe gash with major bleeding, a wound he had probably tried to doctor himself before giving up and coming down to the clinic. I stood up and motioned him toward the treatment room. When he limped around the desk I saw that the right leg of his coveralls was saturated with blood. A trail of wet red boot prints followed him down the tiled hall.

Refusing my help, he hoisted himself onto the table. I quickly cut open his pant leg and stared in bewilderment at the wad of coarse gray material that filled the wide gash running from just above his knee almost to his groin. Then it dawned on me. Spanish moss. He had used fistfuls of Spanish moss to stanch the bleeding.

"Paul!" I yelled down the hall to the clinic physician. "I need you in surgery, now please!"

Dr. Paul Braxton's face registered the same shock and bewilderment as he surveyed the moss-stuffed wound, until understanding dawned. "Son of a bitch," he muttered. At least the moss had done its intended job of stopping the bleeding.

A quick x-ray revealed that the femur, the large thighbone, was still intact. The chainsaw had missed the femoral artery, which was also a blessing, because even the absorbent moss would not have stopped that type of hemorrhage. Before we could suture the wound, however, we would have to clean it, and the brittle moss, which was riddled with chiggers—tiny, blood-sucking insects—was almost impossible to remove.

Armed with tweezers, gauze, spray bottles of saline, and syringes, we set to work, meticulously picking out countless bits of moss, dirt, and debris. Unfortunately, the gash was too large and the chore of cleaning it too slow to allow us to anesthetize it completely.

Paul had initially told the patient that we would only bandage and splint the leg and then send him down to the hospital in Charleston for proper treatment, but he had, predictably, refused. "Hell, I didn't even want to come here!" he snorted. Paul had warned him it would be slow, tedious, and painful work, but the weather-beaten farmer had brushed aside his concern.

"Just do what ya need to do, Doc. It don't matter none to me."

And so we picked, sprayed, wiped, cleaned, and debrided the wound while he lay with gritted teeth but made no sound. It took both of us the better part of an hour to clean the crumbly moss, the crawly chiggers, and the rest of the debris out of the wound and finally sew it up. It took over twenty dissolvable internal stitches and just as many external stitches to close the leg.

When we were done, Dr. Braxton looked at him sternly. "You are not, under any circumstances, to try and take these stitches out yourself. I want to see you here again in ten days, understand?"

The farmer made a wry face.

"Nurse Kate will bandage the wound, and you're to stay off this leg for the next few days."

A wry grin lifted one corner of his mouth. "That ain't gonna happen."

Paul rolled his eyes. He knew how stubborn these independent Lowcountry farmers and shrimpers could be.

"Are you allergic to any medicine?" I asked.

He shook his head. "Why?"

"Because you're not leaving here without a full dose of antibiotics."

"I don't need no antibiotics."

"There was enough dirt and bacteria in that wound to infect half this town," Dr. Braxton barked. "Now don't give Kate a hard time about the shots. I'll see you in ten days." He washed his hands and left the room.

I drew up the penicillin and turned back to the patient.

He groaned. "Two shots? Shoot. Can't I just take some pills?"

"Nope. Now drop those britches, please."

Grudgingly he lowered his pants.

During the early days of my nursing career, antibiotics were at the peak of potency, with each cc of an injection containing about 200 mgs of penicillin. Paul Braxton was one of those physicians who disliked prescribing oral antibiotics because he was convinced that their misuse was going to render these life-saving drugs useless by the turn of the century. Every time a patient started a round of antibiotics for something other than a bacterial infection, or every time a patient felt better just five days into a ten-day antibiotic course and stopped the medication too soon, the problem of antibiotic-resistant bacteria was compounded: Any bacteria remaining in the patient's system when he stopped taking the antibiotics had already been exposed to them and quickly mutated so that any future use of the same antibiotic would prove ineffective.

Although his colleagues often laughed at him, Paul Braxton was unfortunately proven right. By the late 1990s, it took *2 million* units of penicillin per cc to be effective, and by the turn of the century, MRSA, a lethal, antibiotic-resistant strain of staphylococcus, a bug once easily killed by antibiotics, was running rampant in hospitals and even killing patients.

I injected a dose of penicillin into each hip and then watched the patient for an allergic reaction. "Where were you when you did this?" I asked as I finished dressing the wound.

"On Wapataw Island," he answered with a shrug.

Wapataw Island? That was a thirty-minute boat ride up the Intracoastal Waterway from here! "Is that where you got cut?" I asked.

"Uh-huh. Me and m' brother was out there lookin' for a Christmas tree for his kids. They got some good pines growin' near the inlet. Slipped in the mud while I was cuttin' and didn't have nothin' to tie up m' leg, and we still had to haul the tree down to the boat and drop it off at his house first. I figured the moss would hold it till I got here."

"What time did you do this?"

He frowned. "Recon' about ten this mornin'."

I looked at the clock. Two p.m.

Four hours ago. In that time, he had hauled a Christmas tree across the marsh and down the Intracoastal Waterway in his boat, brought his brother home, and then drove himself to the clinic, all the while sporting a horrific injury.

Pressing my lips together, I filled out the paperwork and then discussed the post-surgical instructions, which included elevating the leg and taking it easy for the next forty-eight hours. Not surprisingly, he shook his head.

"Ain't gonna happen. I got me a farm to run, hogs to feed, fences to fix, the whole nine yards. And my brother always needs help with them kids since his wife died last year."

He must have seen the expression on my face, because he smiled and patted my shoulder. "Now don't you worry so much, ma'am. God'll provide and get me through. He always does."

***

I had moved to South Carolina from suburban Connecticut with my family about five years ago. My father was in the military and had been transferred to the navy base in Charleston while my siblings and I were starting high school. This was one of our family's many military moves, so I figured that South Carolina was merely another temporary place to land. But by the time I graduated from high school, my father had decided to retire, and even though he and my mom moved elsewhere, I enrolled in college in South Carolina to take advantage of the low in-state tuition.

When my very Yankee family and I first arrived in the South Carolina Lowcountry, I was shocked by what I considered to be the backwardness of the people and the area. Our brand-new housing development was surrounded by soybean and tomato fields. Sandy roads connected us to the two-lane highway that cut through the fields, and all you could hear day and night was the peeping of frogs and bob-white quail. Our neighbors kept horses. And it was here that I saw my first black widow spider, my first cockroach (called "palmetto bugs" here; most of them were as long as my thumb), and cottonmouth snakes—there were a lot of those around our house.

In the nearby historic city of Charleston, the upper crust "South of Broad Street" natives seemed to be stuck in time—namely that of the Civil War. Confederate flags flew from a lot of houses and cars, and I stared in disbelief the first time I saw an elderly white dowager walking down Meeting Street carrying a fringed silk parasol to shield her from the sun while a black woman weighted down with shopping bags struggled behind her. Every pickup truck seemed to sport a bumper sticker that read something like *We don't care how you did it up north* or *Hell no, we ain't forgettin'*.

Out in the country, away from the gorgeous antebellum houses of Charleston and the plantations on the Ashley River, many of the area's rural homes lacked insulation, heating, and indoor plumbing. It was in South Carolina that I first heard the "N-word" spoken aloud, by an adult, no less, who certainly should have known better. Having grown up in a culturally diverse neighborhood in a vibrant New England town, I was appalled.

Charleston neighborhoods were still segregated—oh, not intentionally, but those big, fancy houses on the historic peninsula were all inhabited by whites; the lower-income folk lived in smaller, more ramshackle houses farther away from the waterfront, and the majority were black. At the all-white private high school my siblings and I attended, I was warned by my peers that the mere idea of a black boy dating a white girl was unthinkable.

The South, my brothers, sister, and I decided, had forgotten to move out of the last century. No surprise then that I planned to bail out of South Carolina as soon as I graduated from college. But over time, and to my utter surprise, I found myself growing to love the Lowcountry. The initial culture shock and my admittedly ill-concealed arrogance toward the "uncultured" and "backward" South Carolinians I lived among gradually gave way to grudging respect and even admiration for their independence, resilience, and resourcefulness.

But it took a while.

***

When I finished my RN at the Medical University of South Carolina, I took a job in Dr. Paul Braxton's clinic while I decided which direction my life should take. Clinic work took a while to get used to after the regimented routine of academia, and being young and ambitious, I was determined to make my mark on this, my first job.

Initially this meant making changes in the way the clinic was run. For instance, the building still had separate "white" and "colored" waiting rooms left over from the pre-civil rights era. Although segregation of this type had long been outlawed, the clinic's black patients still tended to congregate in the waiting room that separated them from the whites. I began my endeavor of bringing about change by turning one of these waiting rooms into a children's waiting room with miniature chairs and tables, toys and books.

Now all adult patients had to wait in the same room together.

It also hadn't taken me long to notice that the senior nurses at the clinic had the abhorrent habit of calling white patients into the examination rooms by using their formal names; however, "Mr. Mayfield, please come with me to room one" was replaced with "Willie, you come to room one" for a black patient. I made a point of respectfully referring to every patient as "Mr." or "Mrs.," "sir," or "ma'am."

Initially it didn't do much for my popularity with the staff, but without realizing it, I was endearing myself to our patients. Gradually, albeit grudgingly, the rest of the staff came along. This was a defining time for me; I was fighting my own little war on prejudice, and I was winning.

At that time we were one of only a few medical clinics in the nearly one hundred miles of forested land that separated the city of Charleston from Myrtle Beach to the north. Not surprisingly, we drew a large percentage of our patient base from the most isolated, rural parts of this area. Patients who came to our clinic often lived in shacks without modern plumbing; many lacked even a grade-school education. Initially I looked upon their "ignorance" with disdain, but once I began to listen to their stories and learn more about their lives, I realized that they were highly educated in many other ways.

From one patient I learned why my humble garden at the apartment I was renting near the beach was a failure and how to coax vegetables and flowers out of the sandy, salty soil in spite of the grinding summer heat. From another I learned how to supplement my meager diet (nurses aren't paid a particularly stellar salary that allows for a lavish food budget) with fresh-caught shrimp, fish, and crab; from still another I was shown how to make the beautiful sweetgrass reed baskets—a skill that had been brought from Africa by slaves and handed down from mother to daughter over generations. It was not until years later that I realized how much I had been taken into that basket weaver's trust, for reed basketry was at that time a closely guarded skill.

Although my misshapen basket could never come close to the beautiful creations sold on street corners in historic Charleston or small roadside stands along the highway leading from Charleston north toward Myrtle Beach, I kept the basket I had made with pride on my kitchen table. When my house burned down almost ten years later, I grieved for its loss.

Sometimes working at the clinic was frustrating or sad, but most often it was joy-filled and rewarding. It gave me an unexpectedly unique opportunity to learn and grow. It humbled me and taught me to see the world through a far wider field of vision.

Of Fathers and Babies

"Angelina, you're pregnant."

"No'm, I ain't."

"Yes, you are."

"Uh-uh."

"Then let me check you for a tumor."

"No sir, and that's final!"

There was no way, absolutely no way Paul Braxton and I were going to get Angelina to admit she was pregnant. This despite her burgeoning belly, the clearly audible fetal heart tones, and the positive pregnancy test. Proper pre-natal care was out of the question; Angelina hitchhiked or walked the fifteen-odd miles from her home near the tiny shrimping village of McClellanville to our clinic for her medical appointments—but only when she deemed it absolutely necessary.

Her mother, Mae, had brought the twenty-three-year-old in now that she was hugely pregnant, and although this was going to be Angelina's fourth child, she was determined not to accept care. Her slightly swollen ankles and somewhat elevated blood pressure made us concerned about pre-eclampsia, a potentially fatal condition in pregnancy.

We begged, we pleaded, we reasoned, we scolded, but Angelina would not budge. There was nothing more Dr. Braxton or I could do. Reluctantly we sent her home with prenatal vitamins and medical orders we doubted she would follow.

About three weeks later, after a particularly long and grueling day at the clinic with both Dr. Braxton and me working very late, I went home and fell into bed utterly exhausted. I was awakened by the ringing of the telephone shortly after midnight.

"Miss Kate? Miss Kate? This is Mae. Angelina, she's havin' this baby right now!"

I clicked on the bedside lamp and cursed under my breath. Still groggy with sleep I sat up. "Can you call the ambulance?"

"Oh, Miss Kate, you know good and well she ain't gonna allow that no way. Y'all send a ambulance here an' she'll disappear into the marsh. You know that as God's truth!"

"Isn't there a local midwife you can call?"

"She ain't speakin' to Angelina."

I sighed heavily. "Okay, okay. I'll call Dr. Braxton."

I phoned Paul, and his wife answered. I explained the situation, and she told me she was sorry, but Paul was on rotation at the hospital in Charleston that night. "You'll just have to call for an ambulance," she told me.

I hung up the phone and buried my face in my hands. Shit, shit, SHIT! No way was I ready to handle a delivery on my own—especially not with a potentially pre-eclamptic patient. But I pulled on my clothes, jumped into my car, and headed north through the dark, empty pine forest.

I could hear Angelina's screams as I pulled up to the small clapboard shack in which she and her mother and children lived. Every one of her children, I knew, had different fathers, and not one of those men had ever come forward to offer financial aid, to help out, to involve themselves in their children's lives. Paul Braxton had once confronted the man who he was sure had fathered Angelina's oldest boy as the resemblance between the two was unmistakable. But when asked, the man had just grinned and responded, "You think I'm Mama's baby-daddy? I dunno. Maybe."

Unfortunately, in those days, if mothers could not or would not reveal the name of the father, their newborns weren't issued a birth certificate, something that would negatively impact the children for the rest of their lives. Thus I and the other nurses in the clinic sometimes spent days trying to determine a father's identity, mostly without success. In those cases Dr. Braxton falsified the information so the child would not suffer from the parents' mistakes.

I stepped out of my car and into the darkness of Angelina's home.

"Heaven help me, Miss Kate! This baby's comin' an' he'll be the death of me!" Angelina was moaning and rocking back and forth on a spindly metal bed. The cabin had that smell I would quickly come to recognize during my time as a social worker as rural poverty: soured milk, wood smoke, and sweat all mixed up in despair. Yet in spite of the poverty, Angelina and Mae's cabin was spotlessly clean.

Angelina's other children had been sent "down the road" to a neighbor; Angelina's mother sat beside her singing a spiritual in a clear alto voice.

I washed my hands in the sulfuric-smelling artesian water that was pumped from an old-fashioned pump handle directly into the kitchen sink. It wasn't much, but it would have to do. I sat down at the end of the bed, lifted the sheet, and parted Angelina's legs. To my horror I saw that a shock of curly brown hair was visible against her bulging perineum. She was already crowning. I took a deep breath.

"It's almost here, Angelina," I said matter-of-factly, my somewhat clipped tone and forced smile covering my underlying terror. I had only been present at the delivery of three other babies, and each time an obstetrician had been in charge. This time I was completely on my own.

Angelina groaned and bore down. There was no time to check her vitals; there was barely time for me to tuck a disposable pad between her legs from the OB kit I had grabbed at the clinic before heading out. The latex gloves in the kit were too big, and I pulled them on clumsily.

"You ever done this before, Miss Kate?" Angelina's mother asked, her intelligent brown eyes peering at me sharply over her glasses. I sensed she could see right through my façade of calm professionalism to the panic beneath.

"Of course!" I smiled. *Well, not on my own*, but I kept that thought to myself. Mae eyed me skeptically but kept on singing.

"You push, you push now, baby," she crooned to her daughter.

I held a washcloth against Angelina's vulva, praying she wouldn't tear. I knew I didn't have the competency to do an episiotomy, a small cut that would prevent a larger vulvar tear as the baby's head emerged. I remembered one of my nursing instructors telling us that counter-compression against the vulva with a warm, wet washcloth could often mitigate tearing. I prayed it would work.

Angelina bore down with super-human strength, grabbed her mother's hands, and screamed.

Then to my amazement she began to sing with her mother: *Swing low, sweet chariot, comin' for to carry me home; swing low, sweet chariot; comin' for to carry me home. I looked over to Jordan and what did I seeeee...*

The *see* was swallowed by another scream, which faded into a primal grunt that was practically ripped from Angelina's chest. The baby's head emerged into my hand. I suctioned its nose and mouth; it was covered in milky vernex, mucus, and blood. The head rotated, and I felt for a cord around the baby's neck. By the grace of God, there was none. I heaved a huge sigh of relief.

"One more push, sweetheart," I encouraged, "one more. What do you want? A boy or a girl?"

"None!" Angelina groaned. "I don't want neither—ohhh!" Another huge push, and a tiny, perfect boy, his skin the color of beautifully polished ebony, slipped into my hands. I was shaking, laughing, and crying at the same time. He was slippery, and I laid him between his mother's legs as I gently toweled him off.

"It's a boy, Angelina," I breathed. "A beautiful baby boy."

At that moment it didn't matter that he had been born into poverty; it didn't matter that he was unwanted by his mother, unknown to his father, and that he'd seemingly started life with the deck stacked against him. I looked down at this perfect little creature, this undeniable reaffirmation that God was not yet tired of us humans, and marveled at his beauty.

He rewarded me by urinating on my shirt.

I laughed and placed him in his mother's arms. In spite of her insistence that she didn't want this child, she pulled him to her and studied his face, counted his fingers and toes, then took him to her breast.

"Ain't he the most beautiful baby you ever seen?"

I smiled at Angelina. "Yes," I said honestly, "he is."

"I can't do much in life," she sighed, "but I sure do make pretty babies!"

***

A week later I accompanied Maryann Tevis, a Child Protective Services social worker, back to Angelina's home. We found Angelina and Mae in the kitchen doing laundry in the rusted sink. The baby was lying in a bassinet sleeping. They had named him Tyrone. I peered into the crib and started when I noticed two small pieces of crossed broom straw resting on his head. Puzzled, I looked at Angelina's mother.

"Oh, that," she said, looking a little embarrassed. "Don't you be mindin' that. That's just keepin' the voodoo away."

"Voodoo culture is pretty widespread in the Lowcountry," Maryann explained, seeing the perplexed look on my face.

While I weighed and measured the baby, Maryann helped Angelina complete the paperwork to include Tyrone in the AFDC (Aid to Families with Dependent Children), food stamps, and other welfare programs. The adrenalin rush of having delivered a baby had long since worn off, and I suddenly found myself not so enamored of another welfare mother delivering another welfare baby, and I said so to Maryann on the way home.

"How can you stand doing what you do?" I fumed in despair. "Now there's another kid born into this world who is going to grow up unemployed, living on SSI and food stamps, who creates more welfare babies for the rest of us to feed, and then vanishes from their lives. 'Mama's baby-daddy? I dunno, maybe' ha!" I snorted.

Maryann smiled patiently. "You can't just abandon people to starve. The solution to poverty is education. 'Give me a fish and I eat for a day, teach me to fish and I eat for a lifetime,'" she quoted. "Kids can't help being born into poverty. If they don't have the resources at home to break out of the cycle, then someone—a teacher, social worker, nurse, neighbor, anyone—needs to step in, to teach them how to change. Sometimes it's as simple as role-modeling."

"And giving them food stamps does that how?" I snapped. "Food and shelter have to come first." Maryann's patience with me was amazing. "That's basic human survival. Getting them into school or counseling is secondary."

I snorted again. "And how many successes have you had?"

"A few. And they're usually your least likely clients."

I looked at Maryann dubiously. She was sixty years old and getting ready to retire. I knew she had been a social worker for almost twenty-five years. I wondered how she could remain so optimistic about her clients—people I felt were stuck in a hopeless generational spiral of poverty.

"They are hopeless," I told her. "They will never break out of this cycle, go to college, or be anything but welfare recipients."

Maryann smiled at me. "Know what?" she said softly. "I used to be one of them."

"One of who?"

"Child of a drug-addicted welfare mother. It was a social worker who changed my life."

I felt the color rising to my face.

Of Witch Doctors and Voodoo Queens

His name was Richard Stratts, and he was both an MD and a trained clinical psychologist. He served as an emergency room physician who specialized in the treatment of patients with psychosomatic conditions that presented themselves in conjunction with a belief in voodoo hexes.

The cases he encountered were almost always the same: a patient, usually from one of the area's more remote islands, would appear in the emergency room with a complaint of severe abdominal pain or, more commonly, chest pains, weakness, and diaphoresis (sweating).

All of them were convinced they were having a heart attack—an AMI (*acute myocardial infarction* in medical terms). Sometimes their EKGs would show mild, benign arrhythmias or, more rarely, a depressed T wave (basically the electrical activity of the heart's ventricles), but usually they were normal.

Still, no amount of explaining could convince the patient that he or she wasn't having a heart attack. The patients would look at us in terror and insist that "the witch doctor" had placed a voodoo hex on them by putting a needle into a doll's chest. And each and every one of them were convinced they were going to die.

Dr. Stratts had figured out long ago that the best way to counter any voodoo-caused "illness" was to kill it with stronger magic. No amount of medication, no placebo, no intensive counseling was ever effective because in the mind of the patient the cause—the witchdoctor's spell—was stronger than any medication or palliative care the hospital could provide.

Rick Stratts's theory? Fight magic with magic.

On this particular evening I was doing an educational rotation in the ER of one of the region's smaller hospitals. I had decided to become an EMT, an emergency medical technician, with the training provided through a new program offered at a local community college. I felt it would supplement my nursing, since "street medicine" emergencies (that is, working accidents in the field) was something I occasionally encountered but felt inadequate to deal with.

That's how I found myself assisting Dr. Rick Stratts. He was a good-looking man with intensely blue eyes and a winning smile. He exuded confidence and caring, and there wasn't a nursing or EMT student in the ER who didn't wish he was single—including me. At least I had been lucky enough to be assigned to his shift.

Now, confronted by a patient whose symptoms he was obviously familiar with, Dr. Stratts pulled me aside and said quietly, "Just go along with what I do."

I nodded in agreement and followed him back into the tiny exam room.

The lab work and EKG had already confirmed that the patient, a terrified woman in her early forties, was not having a heart attack. All other tests performed were within the normal range.

The patient, however, was convinced that she was dying of a heart attack since she had angered not only the witch doctor, but also the "Voodoo Queen" the day before.

"She did it," the woman gasped.

"Did what?" Dr. Stratts asked kindly.

"She put this hex on me! I'm dyin', oh my Lord, I'm dyin'!"

"Are you quite sure?" he asked, still sounding endlessly gentle and patient.

"Oh Lord, I'm sure!"

"Mrs. Friedman," Dr. Stratts said calmly but authoritatively, "the only way to help you is to undo the magic, and I can do that. But you have to help me, do you understand?"

Mrs. Friedman eyed the doctor skeptically. "How you gonna do that? You can't undo a voodoo hex!"

"I can, and I will," he answered. "I studied counter-spells when I worked in hospitals in Africa, Asia, and the Caribbean. Either you believe me or you don't. It's up to you."

Mrs. Friedman closed her eyes and moaned. "I got no choice, I guess. I'm dyin' anyway. You do what you can."

Dr. Stratts smiled reassuringly. "All right then, let's begin." He opened a cabinet and pulled out some supplies: a candle, a cardboard cut-out of a cross, a cardboard cut-out of a five-pointed star, matches, and what looked like a whisk made of local sawgrass.

He turned to the patient, who had stopped moaning and was watching him, fascinated—as was I.

"What I need is one of your hairs. The most powerful hairs come from your pubis; the ones on your head work, but they're not as strong. You decide which you want me to use."

The patient looked thoughtful, then reached down and plucked a pubic hair from her groin and placed it in Dr. Stratts's gloved hand. He smiled. "Good."

He placed the star on the counter nearest the exam table, laid the cross over that, and then balanced the candle on the center of the cross. Next he motioned for me to turn off the lights.

When it was dark, he lit the candle then dropped the hair into the flame. A singed, acrid smell filled the room.

Dr. Stratts picked up the whisk, which he held like a wand, and began waving it over the flame. He then turned to the patient and waved it over her chest.

"Now repeat after me," he ordered. He uttered some words that sounded like complete nonsense to me; they could have been Swahili or Mandarin or Tagalog or just made-up sounds for all I knew. I was too mystified to think about it—or to laugh.

The patient began to repeat the words with the doctor, over and over, faster and faster, until he shouted, "Be GONE!" He blew out the candle and the room was plunged into darkness.

Silence.

Presently Dr. Stratts said, "Turn on the light, please."

I groped for the switch. He stepped up to Mrs. Friedman's bed, placed his stethoscope in his ears, and made a great show of listening to her chest.

After a full minute he smiled. "It worked," he said softly.

For a moment the patient lay stunned, then tears welled in her eyes. "Oh, praise be to God! Praise the Lord! Amen! Amen! Amen!"

Rick Stratts patted the patient's hand and instructed me to help her dress.

Her follow-up care was to burn another hair every night for a week and to utter a prayer for health and protection from dark magic with it. He also gave her a bottle of pills with the instructions to take one every night for a month.

"I promise you," he said gravely, "not only will it undo the hex completely, but it will prevent the witch doctor or any voodoo queen from ever being able to hex you again."

After she left, I asked him what the pills were. He grinned. "Vitamins."

***

Exactly one week later I found myself working again on Rick Stratts's shift. It was a slow night and the emergency room was thankfully quiet.

Toward ten o'clock the ER doors opened and a woman stormed in. I had never seen anyone quite like her. She was tall, just over six feet, and her rich black hair was streaked with brilliant orange dye. She wore dozens of bangles around her neck, on her ankles, on her wrists.

She was dressed in a brightly colored broom skirt layered with numerous blouses of jewel-bright colors and the most outlandish hat I had ever seen, resplendent with multicolored feathers.

She headed straight for the doctor. "You!" she hissed. "You!"

Rick Stratts stopped in the middle of the hall holding a clipboard, his head slightly cocked.

I knew immediately who this must be. The Voodoo Queen. The few other nurses and orderlies in the hallway stopped dead in their tracks.

"You!" she hissed again, circling Rick, her arms waving like snakes, up and down, up and down. "You! Undo my spells? Oh no, no one undoes Queen Bereniece's magic, no one! How dare you? How dare you?"

A security officer moved toward the woman, but Rick motioned him away.

"My magic is stronger than yours," he said levelly.

"Nobody's magic is stronger than mine!" she screeched. "*Nobody's*!"

She stopped her dance and glared at him. "I will hex you; I will put a killing curse on you if you ever, ever do that again!"

"My magic is stronger than yours," he repeated.

"Bah!" she spat. She made a few more motions with her arms, as if she was gathering dust up into them. Then she flung this "armful" in our direction, turned, and stalked toward the exit.

She stopped at the door. "We'll see!" she hissed. "We'll see!" With that she turned and left the hospital.

I stood there with my mouth open. Everyone else stared, goggle-eyed.

Dr. Stratts looked at each one of us, shrugged, grinned, and headed down the hall. "That's what she told me last time too."

When my shift ended I went home and burned one of my pubic hairs. Not that I believed in voodoo dust, mind you, but what could it hurt?

Hypothermia in the Deep South

It was the last hour of my ER shift. The night had been surprisingly quiet. Only one patient, a "gobbler" who was well known to the staff, had come in screaming that his leg was broken. A gobbler is a patient who suffers from a series of psychosomatic complaints. Most of these individuals are lonely and turn to medical providers for human contact. Others are mentally ill and truly believe they're suffering from a variety of maladies.

This individual had reportedly fallen from his roof (in the middle of the night?) but showed no signs of injury. Still, the ambulance crew had brought him in for the ER staff to evaluate. The patient insisted that his leg was broken. X-rays revealed strong, healthy bones, and while a resident distracted the patient, the orthopedist wrenched firmly on the patient's leg. He never even flinched.

"Go home, Jerry," the doctor sighed. "Next time don't come back unless you're really hurt."

Jerry looked prepared to argue, then shrugged and headed out of the emergency room door.

"That's three times this week," the triage nurse said, shaking her head.

"What do you do with patients like that?" I asked her.

"Turn them over to the social workers. Sometimes they can help, sometimes not."

By then I had worked with Maryann Tevis long enough to know that she and her agency struggled badly with very limited resources. Maryann once told me that trying to help all her families was akin to bailing out the marsh with a tin cup. "But sometimes, sometimes we can make a huge difference."

I thought of Maryann later that evening when the ambulance crew brought in a handsome elderly gentleman with gray hair. He was so thin his ribs showed clearly, and he was unconscious.

"EMTs found him in his living room—neighbors said they hadn't seen him in a few days. The room was below freezing; there's no heat, no insulation, and no food in the refrigerator."

"Freezing to death in his own living room?" As a child of central heat and air conditioning, raised by a mother who had cooked enormous meals every day, I could not fathom anyone succumbing to starvation or hypothermia in their own home. I was stunned. We warmed him, and by the time my shift was over he was awake but groggy and I wheeled him upstairs to be admitted.

The next day I went to visit him. He was propped up in bed reading a newspaper, and he looked up and smiled when I entered. "Hi, Mr. Rivers, I'm Kate. I was in the ER when you came in last night."

The smile widened into a toothy grin. He invited me to sit down, and I perched on the chair beside his bed.

Mr. Rivers was a talker, and once he got going, he didn't stop. I learned that he had been married; his wife had died a few years ago and he still missed her terribly. They had two children, a son and a daughter. He had been raised by a single mother, the son of an alcoholic, abusive father who showed up just long enough to impregnate his wife again and again and beat his children before leaving.

When Mr. Rivers turned sixteen, he ran away. World War I was raging overseas, and he enlisted by lying about his age and served with the infantry in France. In World War II his military experience eventually landed him with the Tuskegee Airmen, and he ultimately served as a bomber escort in Europe. After the war his military pension ran out quickly, and he took a job in a farm equipment factory. He finished high school on a military grant and was determined that his own children would have a better life. He and his wife, a domestic worker, scrimped and saved and managed to send both children to college. He was immensely proud of them. I learned that his wife's illness had drained them of every penny they had. With no pension and too proud to turn to his children for help, he soon became destitute.

The unit charge nurse arranged for an Adult Protective Services social worker to visit with Mr. Rivers. I was amazed at the services that were put in place for him. Weekly visits from a home-health nurse were started, and SSI (Social Security's Supplemental Income program), disability income, food stamps, and Medicare were procured. The social worker then arranged for a church group to help insulate Mr. Rivers's house. When Mr. Rivers protested that he was not about to accept "charity," the social worker quietly pointed out that he had not only served his country but had paid taxes for many, many years.

"It's about time you get some of that money back," he told him.

But to me the most important thing that this young social worker gave Mr. Rivers was dignity and respect. I left the hospital with my head spinning. I began to see that welfare was not always the dead-end, endless "dole" I had believed it to be. I had now seen social workers like Maryann and that Adult Protective Services worker strive to find solutions to poverty. Welfare came with requirements for education and job training. It offered everything from a way up and out for single mothers to end-of-life dignity for seniors like Mr. Rivers.

As a nurse I was seeing dozens of patients whose illnesses originated with poverty. The medical teams could treat their bodies, but I was beginning to feel that this was like putting a Band-Aid over a tumor. The causes—poverty and ignorance and often circumstances beyond anyone's control—remained.

The next morning I called Maryann Tevis and we had breakfast together. I shared with her what I was feeling, and she smiled.

"Being a social worker has been one of the most rewarding things I've ever done with my life," she told me. "I haven't regretted it for a moment." She studied my face. "Kate," she said at last, "I know you're young and the future feels like forever. But don't wait. Do the things that matter now. Climb those mountains; grab every opportunity you can. You can make a difference. Do it. Don't be afraid to change, to try new things."

Two months later Maryann and her husband retired and followed their dream. They purchased a motor home and took off to see America. A month later, Dr. Braxton and I received word that they had been killed in a wreck somewhere in Mississippi.

Even during my grief, Maryann's words stuck with me. I loved nursing, and I knew that eventually I would want to come back to it. But something was calling me to change, to do more than suture up wounds, deliver babies, and give shots. That fall I enrolled in the MSW (master of social work) program at Emory University in Atlanta, Georgia. Two years later I was hired with Child Protective Services in the small rural town of Highton, North Carolina, in the heart of the Appalachian Mountains.

Marsha Braun – the Worst Client EVER

"I'll start you off with an easy case." Hilary Bench, the CPS unit supervisor, slid a blue intake sheet in my direction. "Young mother, name of Marsha; four children, living in a car. You just need to find them a place to live, get her on food stamps and AFDC, try to locate the father(s), and be sure the children are enrolled in school."

"Sure!" I answered cheerfully. "Piece of cake."

Marsha was my first CPS client. She was also my worst. Four years after our first interview, she was still on my caseload. Drug addicted, in denial, resistant to treatment, I saw her as utterly hopeless. Worse, a string of defense attorneys continued to fight everything I tried to get Marsha to do that might change her life. Her children, aged three months to six years, had been removed from her care shortly after I took on the case, but because the situation never went into "permanency planning" (severance of all parental ties and subsequent adoption) and the goal was still to "rehabilitate and reunite" the family, the case remained on my desk, and I hated it.

Marsha took up an inordinate amount of my time—hours and hours, in fact, between arranging what I deemed to be useless therapy appointments because she never attended them, court appearances that dragged on forever, drug screening, parenting classes, job training. Anything and everything I could think of and tried, failed. Marsha resisted me at every turn. She hated me as much as I hated working with her. I lost count of the number of staff review case studies that were presented on this family; I pleaded with my supervisor to turn her case over to another worker, but to no avail. Hilary staunchly refused to take Marsha off my hands.

I began to doubt my decision to give up nursing for social work, but Hilary was encouraging. She echoed the words Maryann Tevis had once said to me.

"Don't be so impatient, Kate. Changes come slowly, but they come. Give your clients, and yourself, a chance."

Grudgingly I stuck it out with Marsha. I arranged for the court-ordered police escorts to pick Marsha up from home (often she was in a drunken stupor) and drag her into court or a therapist's office. I dogged her, nagged her, dragged her out of bed and out of bars. She screamed that I was embarrassing her and ruining her life. I drove her to counseling appointments and home again only to have her curse and berate me the entire way. In spite of Hilary's words, I knew Marsha Braun was beyond help.

One thing remained certain, however. Marsha loved her children. Unfortunately, she loved being high even more. But somehow she managed to never miss a visit with them, and she even managed to show up for those visits sober. I didn't attribute this to any strength of character on her part, however. I attributed it to the fact that I had told her that her visits with her children would be curtailed if she was drunk or high. I used permanent severance as a threat, reunification as a bribe; meanwhile, I pulled out my hair in frustration.

Then finally, finally, after four years on my caseload, she moved to another county. Never had I been so overjoyed to transfer out a case. Marsha's parting comment to me at our last meeting was "good riddance, bitch!"

I'd be lying if I said I didn't want to slap her. I thought of Maryann Tevis as I watched Marsha go.

"Where are all the successes you told me about, Maryann?" I sighed aloud. "It seems all that lands in my caseload are failures."

A String of Failures

As part of my graduate studies I specialized in child neglect cases. Usually these translated to "dirty house" calls. Teachers concerned about children who came to school inappropriately dressed for the weather, dirty, smelly, and inevitably without homework or lunches would call Child Protective Services (CPS). Child neglect can encompass physical or emotional aspects; issues such as medical, dental, nutrition, and education all fall into this category. In some cases the cause is simple ignorance and poverty; in many more cases the cause is drug addiction and alcoholism.

For the simpler cases, the involvement of a home-help worker is often adequate. These dedicated and underpaid women and men go into a home and teach a parent how to cook, clean, and run a household. Neglectful parents are often overwhelmed or depressed. Some are too poor to buy groceries, pay bills, or afford even the simplest medical care. Very few of them know where to turn for help, and most, I learned, had never been nurtured themselves. No wonder the pattern perpetuated itself.

Fortunately, child neglect cases rarely went into permanency planning. Usually support services such as food stamps and AFDC, home-help and counseling were adequate, and after a few months the case could be closed.

A few families were far more difficult, however, and it was not uncommon for child neglect to cover a more serious and insidious problem such as child sexual assault. With time I would shift my area of expertise and become a child sexual assault specialist. One such case was the Mertz family...

***

The Mertzes lived in an old clapboard farmhouse up a long dirt road at the apex of a hollow—a valley between remote hilltops deep in rural Appalachia that the locals referred to as a "holler." It was all I could do to get my ancient, wheezing Volkswagen with questionable brakes up the rutted dirt road that led to their farm.

The intake complaint had come from the school. The Mertz children, thirteen-year-old twins, rarely attended school. When they did, they were filthy and smelled terrible, often of feces. Their teeth were rotten, their hair was filled with lice and nits, and they were obese.

Although I was almost always able to establish a good rapport with the children I interviewed, my encounter with the Mertz twins at school had been unsettling; they were sullen, angry, and resistive. The school guidance counselor told me that when the children first came to the school, having been forced to attend after an investigation of their home by a truancy officer, they had no idea what a flush toilet was or how to use it.

Social work interviewing is a critical skill when dealing with resistive families. A good worker needs to know how to gently coax information out of an individual while remaining unbiased, professional, and supportive. The social worker needs to win the family's trust, and so far I had usually been able to do this. With the Mertzes I was the enemy from the start, and it only got worse from there.

On the morning of my first home visit, I picked my way carefully across the Merztes' yard. It was littered with rusting cars, rags, discarded clothing, shoes, bottles, and parts of what looked like an old moonshine still. Chickens perched on the coils protruding from an old mattress. There was a crooked wooden outhouse with the door hanging off the hinges standing next to what appeared to be an old well.

The yard smelled sourly of rotting garbage and feces. Walking across it, I felt as if I had stepped back a hundred years in time.

I could feel, but not see, someone watching my approach from a smeared brown upstairs window. The banjo music from the movie *Deliverance* suddenly flashed through my mind, and I wished fervently that I had brought someone with me.

No doubt Mr. Mertz would have the requisite sawed-off shotgun with him when he met me—and he didn't disappoint. About ten feet from the screened porch, a tall, robust man dressed in filthy coveralls and worn leather boots confronted me. He carried that sour, smoky smell of poverty about him, and he looked mean.

He was holding a sawed-off shotgun, which was cracked open and balanced across his arm—not pointing at me, but certainly giving me a clear message.

"What the hell you want?"

"Hello, Mr. Mertz," I said as cheerfully as I could. I smiled at him but did not extend my hand—I had learned from embarrassing experience that this gesture only drew a disdainful stare. "My name is Kate and I'm with Child Protective Services."

He spat a mouthful of "chaw" or "baccy" (chewing tobacco) on the ground, his small eyes glaring at me. Then to my surprise, he shrugged and motioned for me to come inside.

The house was even filthier than the yard. I had to squeeze around towers of yellowed newspapers and bags of rotting trash. We crossed the kitchen, where stacks of unwashed dishes filled the sink, counters, and table. There were rotting bits of food everywhere, and rodent pellets littered the floor.

In all my years of social work, I had never encountered a house this bad. The smell was overpowering. It was all I could do not to cover my nose and retch.

Abel, the male twin, was standing at the refrigerator. It was wide open, and I could see ropes of mold and fungus hanging like stalactites inside. The refrigerator was empty save for some beer cans and a plate of some disgusting gray glop. Abel turned to stare at me, hatred in his eyes.

"Esther, get your ass down here! We got another one of them social workers on our backs!"

Mr. Mertz sat down on a torn sofa. He did not offer me a seat, and I remained standing near the doorway—a safety tactic taught by the local sheriff in our field safety class. I made a quick mental note of my exits and what obstacles might keep me from reaching them.

Jessica, the female twin, sidled into the room, a drumstick dangling from her fingers.

"What'd I tell you about eatin' between meals?" her father roared. "Give me that thing!"

Jessica ignored her father, sat down on the other end of the sofa, and kept eating. She was hugely overweight, as was her brother. Her clothes were even filthier than they had been when I'd interviewed her at school the day before, and she smelled.

Mrs. Mertz waddled into the room. She too was obese. She could not have been more than forty, but her hair was prematurely gray and her face was drawn and lined. She looked much older than her age.

"You ain't got no business here, woman."

"Mr. and Mrs. Mertz, I'm with Child Protective Services. I'm going to be your caseworker. We've opened a case on you for child neglect. Do you understand what that means?"

"It means you're fucking nosy and should mind your fucking business," Abel snarled, coming to sit beside his sister and snatching the chicken leg from her.

She slapped him, and he punched her back.

Good God, I thought, *what a family!*

"We can work together voluntarily," I continued, ignoring Abel's comment, "or we can work through court order. The choice is yours. In any event, you're stuck with me. My job is to assess your situation, decide what's best to help you, and work with you to clean up this place and your kids and help them do better in school."

"We don't need no help." The snarl came from Esther Mertz. "And we don't need the kind of trouble you're gonna cause us."

"We need to be clear on one thing," I said firmly, holding eye contact with Mrs. Mertz. "I am not the cause of your problems. I'm the result. You can work with me or you can work against me. My job is to keep your family together, but in order to do so there are things that need to be fixed—that we need to work on together to fix."

I paused. "If you won't cooperate, then we go to court and they will create your care plan. You will then be under court order to work with me. I'd rather we work without that kind of pressure." Mr. Mertz snorted. "Whatever you say, woman, whatever you say."

"Do you understand what I'm telling you?" I asked as politely as I could.

"I ain't stupid!"

"I didn't say you were."

All four of the Mertzes sat glaring at me. As calmly as I could, I pulled out a notebook and camera, explained that I needed to keep records, and started to take some photos.

Mr. Mertz immediately got up, took the camera out of my hand, snapped open the back, and pulled out the film.

"Git out," he said. "Now."

I sighed. "I understand. You realize this means we'll have to go to court."

"I don't give a shit."

I nodded, bid them farewell, and made my way as quickly as I could to the car. I didn't breathe a sigh of relief until I was bouncing down the road back to the highway. En route to the office I stopped at my house, tore off my clothes, and threw them in the washer. I showered the stench of the Mertzes' home out of my hair.

This was not an auspicious beginning.

***

I returned to the Mertz home the next day accompanied by a deputy. The officer stood by glumly as I took photographs, wrote field notes, and talked with the family. He kept his eyes down; clearly he was not comfortable with my violation of this family's privacy. I didn't like it either.

I outlined to the Mertzes what I wanted to do: implement the services of a home-help educator, provide them with AFDC and food stamps, enroll Mr. and Mrs. Mertz in parenting classes and the children in therapy. Not surprisingly, the Mertzes refused.

A family court hearing was set for the following week.

Family Court under Judge John Dawley

Judge John Dawley's court was unlike any I had ever been in. Courts can be intimidating for anyone, and it was no different for me as a young woman and a brand-new social worker.

In the early years of my career, I made countless mistakes on the witness stand. I lost my temper, got lulled into an "off the record" conversation with a defense attorney, allowed other attorneys to trip me up on the bench, and overall proved to be a miserable witness.

But I learned.

I learned so well, in fact, that many of the defense attorneys who knew me would take the approach of "voir diring" me, as we called it, on the witness stand. (In the United States, *voir dire* refers to, among other things, questioning expert witnesses about their backgrounds and qualifications. In my courtroom appearances, when I was on the witness stand, it meant trying to make me look incompetent.)

Whenever the attorneys did this, however, I was usually relieved. It almost always meant their clients didn't have a case and that the attorneys' only recourse was to try and discredit me. Rather than being upset or angered by the intimidation and insinuations that inevitably were thrown at me in court, I would calmly and quietly bat them back.

I knew I had really succeeded one morning when I overheard a public defender talking to one of my clients outside the courtroom during recess.

"Kate Jacobs is a reasonable woman. She doesn't know you and has no reason to lie about you. She works hard to keep families together. It would be so much easier for all of us if you just worked with her!"

Libby, the public defender who was speaking, looked up just then and realized I had overheard. She shot me a sheepish grin.

Later she took me aside and warned, "Don't you go getting swell-headed on me. That's the last thing we need."

Fortunately, most judges were reasonable and fair, and I learned that if a judge seemed to be leaning in the parents' favor and allowing them a great deal of liberty in court, he or she inevitably ruled on CPS; that is, on my side.

Judge John Dawley's court, however, was, as they say, "a whole 'nother ballgame."

Judge John Dawley did not wear robes. He wore jeans, a plaid flannel shirt even on the hottest days of the year, and cowboy boots. A tall, white-haired man somewhere in his fifties, he sat up on the dais in a rocking chair with his feet propped on a stool.

Even when court was in session he chewed tobacco, which he spat into a bronze spittoon that he kept on the floor next to the chair. He spoke with a heavy drawl, his speech interspersed with plenty of pauses to take aim at the spittoon. He rarely went along with the recommendations of any social worker, and needless to say, we all hated him.

A typical Judge Dawley response to, say, an allegation of assault would be to put his hands behind his head, tip back in his chair, spit out his chaw, and drawl, "Waahl, Joseph—that's a right good Christian name, by the way—ah kin see the social worker's point. Ah understand ya gotta keep control of yer kids. I understand that kids need the occasional smack with a hickory, but (spit) chainin' yer son to the porch rail while ya smack him with a shovel is a bit on the extreme."

Judge Dawley would then stop and eye the guilty parent. "So tell you (spit) what! You promise you ain't gonna do that agin, and I'll order this here social worker to git off yer back. Fair?"

The guilty parent always thought this was more than fair. I lost track of the number of children Judge Dawley sent back into abysmal situations.

Whenever a parent beat his or her child again, the judge would respond with, "Well, Miss Social Worker, I see that as a call for help. Now y'all go ahead and get those services of yours in place..."

But invariably, no matter what we did, he would close out the case prematurely.

The Mertzes' investigation would have gone as badly except for a surprising allegation from their daughter, Jessica.

After my visit to their home, Jessica went to her guidance counselor at school and told her that she wanted to work with me. She said her father beat both her and her brother regularly, and she lifted her shirt to reveal a series of welts caused by a hickory stick on her back.

Jessica then admitted to the guidance counselor that her father had been forcing her to have sex with him on a regular basis.

A forensic physical exam revealed a perforated hymen and semen samples. Mr. Mertz was arrested and jailed. Jessica and her brother were placed in foster homes, and the case moved to a permanency-planning worker.

Abel Mertz was present during the hearing, and when the judge ordered him to remain in foster care, his eyes narrowed and he glared in my direction. Later, as he passed me in the hall, he spat, "You ruined my family, lady. I'll see you rot in hell."

I for one was immensely relieved to be rid of the case. And once again I couldn't help but think of Maryann Tevis and muse, "Where are the successes you always told me about?"

By now I was feeling pretty hopeless.

Of Mountains and Machismo

Peter Jacobs and I met in graduate school. He was earning his MBA while I was finishing my MSW. After graduating, I knew I didn't want to practice social work in a big city, so I accepted the position with Child Protective Services in the small, mountainous town of Highton, North Carolina.

Peter had accepted a position with a bank in the city of Asheville, a lengthy drive away, and we tried to visit each other on weekends as often as we could. Asheville was about as "big city" as Peter could handle, and we began looking for a place to live that would minimize our long commutes.

We were married in the county justice's office a few months after graduating, honeymooned with a paddling trip down the Chattooga River, and then purchased our first home: a rundown single-story clapboard farmhouse on seven acres that sat halfway between each of our jobs. It meant an almost hour-long drive for both of us in opposite directions, but it afforded Peter relief from the crush of the city and me some badly needed distance between my CPS clients and my private life.

I loved our little farm, and we spent whatever time we could taming the wilderness after years of neglect in order to plant a garden. Cutting back kudzu vines—an invasive plant that leaves trees and telephone poles in the Southeast looking like green dinosaurs—we discovered an assortment of peach and apple trees, as well as a stately black walnut that bombed our cars with large, hard nuts. The nuts would also fall onto our roof, often waking us up with loud clunks.

Peter hated the tree, but I loved it. It was at least a hundred years old, provided wonderful shade in the hot summer, and the walnuts were delicious. My co-workers happily paid us $2 for a large bag—which they harvested themselves. It was, in my opinion, win-win, even though Peter grumbled.

Many happy weekends were spent painting and fixing up the early 1900s house. The only problem was that it was nearly impossible to heat. We hired a contractor to see about insulating it, but he came away from the early inspection shaking his head. The house had been insulated with mud, straw, and burlap sacking, which would be impossible to remove. It was no surprise that several families of field mice set up housekeeping in the walls, but they seemed to stay out of the house itself, so we left them alone.

When we weren't working on the farm, Peter and I spent our weekends either on the river, paddling, or else hiking or making the long drive to Linville Gorge to go rock-climbing. Our passion for outdoor sports is what had drawn us together in the first place. Wanting to keep up my medical skills, I also signed up with the Highton Volunteer Fire Department as an EMT.

Not too long after I started working there, word got back to the captain that I was a "rock jock," and one day he asked if I would be willing to help the department form a local technical rock rescue group.

I agreed.

From February through May of the first year of my marriage, I alternated between my CPS job, volunteering at the fire station, and pulling together a technical rescue unit. I was given a surprisingly large budget for purchasing equipment: ropes, the newest technical ascenders, litter baskets, helmets, and harnesses—you name it and we were able to get it.

I asked a fellow climber, a former Yosemite guide named Beth, to help. We hired recruits and spent weekends refining our techniques in teaching them how to climb, rappel, evacuate injured climbers, and all the other skills needed to become top-notch technical rescue experts.

The program was ready to be officially launched in early June, and we put out the word that we were ready to accept our first students. The training program, or "mountain rescue academy," as we called it, would be held for a week at the base camp of one of the many outdoor sporting centers prevalent in North Carolina, with me and Beth team-teaching with the camp's staff. Our first students were all men.

The entire week was truly rewarding and a lot of fun. By the end of it, we had formed firm friendships with our students, and the Highton EMT captains, Dilly Bracks and Martin Dodds, admitted (after a few too many beers one night) that most of the men in the class were at least a little bit in love with Beth and me.

Apparently that counted for little, however, because when the first calls came in for technical rescue assistance following the training, those EMTs at the fire station who had attended the training always responded, but they never called either Beth or me to assist. We figured that's because we were women—the weaker sex, of course.

But that changed one night when my phone rang shortly after dark. It was Martin. He sounded a bit chagrined.

"Um, Kate, would you, um, mind meeting us at the parking lot to Parson's Mountain? We, um, have a situation up there."

I asked for details, but he was vague. I agreed to respond, hung up, and called Beth.

"Yeah, he called me too," she said, "but he wouldn't say what's up."

Thirty minutes later I pulled into the trailhead parking lot to find it filled with EMS vehicles. A sheepish Martin approached Beth and me and filled us in. It seemed a young woman had fallen from the trail on Parson's Mountain a few hours ago, landing on a ledge about two thousand feet above the valley floor. Two of the EMTs Beth and I had trained had rappelled down to rescue her, but something had gone very wrong. Both men fell and were now sitting on the ledge along with their victim, injured themselves—though fortunately not badly—and unable to help her.

Despite the seriousness of the situation, I had to bite back the "told you so" that hovered on my lips, and I swear I heard Beth choke back a snort of derisive laughter.

Martin looked so woebegone that we took pity on him and didn't say a word. Instead we gathered around the mountain's route map in the back of the rescue rig for a briefing.

Martin pointed up the steep face of the mountain to where the trio was huddled. Luckily the ledge was not far off one of the basic rock-climbing routes both Beth and I used whenever we climbed Parson's Mountain.

The weather was good; it was a mild, dry night with a brilliant array of stars, and Martin briefed us that both the EMTs who had fallen had adequate supply packs that included blankets, food, and water. Their injuries were minor: both had radioed down that they had ankle and shoulder injuries respectively and that the patient, a healthy woman in her twenties, had dislocated her knee in the fall but was otherwise stable.

Because Beth was by far the better, more experienced climber, I deferred team leadership to her. Beth took charge of the situation quickly and easily. She chose a team of six of the best climbers (including me, which did my ego a world of good).

Our task was simple: we would hike up a steep forest trail to a point about fifty feet above the cliff face where the group was stranded. At this level there was a small rock outcropping—not quite a ledge, but large enough for good toe-holds and the ability to place protection in the rock. We would then set up our lines and rappel to the group below. From the ledge we would then rig up a secondary belay system and lower both the men and the patient to another, larger ledge some hundred feet below them. This ledge was known by climbers as the "catwalk" and was accessible by traversing across the cliff-face from a hiking trail on the side. Once there, we would traverse the trio back to the trail and carry them out.

It took us a little over an hour to hike to the upper ledge. We kept in touch with the two injured EMTs by radio, and they could pinpoint our position above them by following our headlamps.

Beth quickly and skillfully set to working hooking up a belay system that consisted of two sit harnesses for each of the injured EMTs and a Stokes litter for the woman. I was impressed with the amount of ropes, carabiners, and figure eight descenders, as well as the then state-of-the-art belay-and-lowering device that Beth set up. Beth planned to remain on the higher ledge supervising the rope work and the lowering system.

Although I had taught with Beth, this system was far more complicated than anything I had ever seen, and I marveled at her setup ability and skill. So too did the men who were working with us. None of them had ever done big rock faces, while Beth had been at home in Yosemite for years—she jokingly referred to Half Dome as her personal climbing wall.

It took the better part of another hour before the system was secured and Beth was satisfied with its safety. At last we clipped in, re-checked our belays, and lowered ourselves to the ledge with the injured climbers. Beth and the remaining pair of rescuers handled the belays and ensured that the system did not snare. Martin, Dilly, and their team were in position on the "catwalk" below, where they had set up for the traverse that would allow them to pull the two injured men and the woman off the rock face and into the forest.

The system worked without a hitch, except that it was very crowded on the ledge. When we reached them, the two EMTs sheepishly told us that they had miscalculated the length of their rappelling ropes and had failed to secure the base. As a result, when they reached the end of the rope, they slid down the rock face for about fifteen feet, landing hard on the ledge beside the woman they'd come to rescue. One had twisted his ankle in the fall, the other had slid past the ledge and lunged for it, luckily catching himself but dislocating his shoulder in the process.

It was almost dawn when we rendezvoused with Martin and his crew on the catwalk, and from there it was a basic carry-out to the waiting ambulances. A grinning Beth and I coiled our ropes and hung up the gear in the rescue rig. On the way back to the station the guys treated us to breakfast at a local pancake house, a high honor indeed. There were toasts made all around for the success of the rescue, razzing of the EMTs, who had "obviously not done a lick of listenin' to their fine instructors," Dilly added, toasting us with his coffee.

From that day on, Beth and I had the respect—and friendship—of all the members of Highton Fire and Rescue, and we were always among the first to be paged for a technical rescue mission. Dilly and Martin became regular visitors at Pete's and my home, and the usually silent and withdrawn Dilly invited us frequently to the lake for a day on his houseboat.

Dilly and Beth were married the following autumn in the park at the base of Parson's Mountain. It was a true mountain wedding, the makeshift altar resplendent with bunches of wildflowers, the sound of banjo and dulcimer music bouncing from the cliff walls, folk dancing, and Dilly's mother frying up a huge platter of catfish and fresh crawdads that Dilly's father had caught in the icy creek that flowed through their yard.

A Silver Bubble

Not long after our move to the farmhouse, Pete and I became close friends with a colleague from his work, Stephan, and Stephan's wife, Virginia. The four of us loved whitewater canoeing and rock climbing, and we spent many happy summer weekends paddling on the French Broad River or scrambling up the cliffs in Linville Gorge.

Virginia had recently graduated from college with a degree in sociology and was looking for work. I suggested that she apply to Highton Social Services, and she managed to land a job in the welfare division. Since she and Stephan lived even farther from the office, Virginia drove to our little farmhouse every morning, then carpooled with me to work. I usually drove because Virginia's car was even older and more unreliable than my 1969 VW.

One morning as the two of us piled into my "bug," one of my contact lenses blew out. A hasty search of my bathroom revealed that I didn't have a spare lens, so Virginia offered to drive. Peter and I lived on a quiet country lane that ended in a "T" at one of the rural highways that connected Highton to the state's larger roads. It was pouring down rain and I cautioned Virginia that many of the puddles on our road hid potholes large enough to swallow the bug.

As we approached the T intersection, Virginia suddenly screamed, "Kate! We don't have brakes!"

It took a moment for her comment to register. "Try pumping them," I suggested quickly, "and turn into the field!"

But Virginia panicked and froze. I looked up, and to my horror I saw that we were already hurtling past the stop sign and onto the highway—right into the path of an oncoming school bus. It was obvious that the bus couldn't stop in time and that we were going to crash.

Aware that school buses weren't equipped with seat belts, all I remember thinking was, *The children! Oh God! Not the children!*

The VW did not have seat belts either, and this was long before the days of airbags. All I could do was close my eyes and throw my arms over my face.

There was a tremendous explosion then the sound of shattering glass and the shrill tearing of metal. I waited for the impact with the windshield, but it didn't come.

Instead I suddenly found myself encased in what can best be described as a bubble—a beautiful silver bubble. Moonlight doesn't describe it; starlight perhaps comes close.

And then I heard a voice—not a thought, but a voice—a male voice, clear and gentle: "Don't be afraid," it said. "You are going to be all right."

How can this be? I thought. *I'm in a bubble and I'm not hitting anything!*

***

Several nights before that I'd had a dream. In it I was sitting in a blue chair in the middle of a highway in the rain, talking to my three paramedic friends, Martin, Jimmy, and Dilly. I had woken up laughing at the ludicrous impossibility of the dream. How could any of us ever get together in one place—while I was sitting on a blue chair on an asphalt road, no less—especially since Martin and Dilly worked miles away for Highton County and Jimmy was an EMT in coastal South Carolina? I attributed the dream to the fact that Jimmy, my former EMT trainer, had been planning to come up to visit us for a few days with his wife, Anne. In fact, they had arrived late yesterday evening.

When I came to after the impact, I found myself sitting on the VW's passenger seat—outside. The seat had broken loose during the impact and bounced out of what was left of the car and was now sitting on the highway. Bending over me were the concerned faces of my three paramedic friends: Jimmy, Dilly, and Martin.

In those days prior to cell phones, help couldn't be summoned quickly.

Luckily there had been a witness to the wreck, and he had gotten out of his car and run to the nearest house, which happened to be mine. Jimmy and Anne had been sitting in the kitchen having breakfast with Pete.

Informed that a wreck had just occurred on the highway, Jimmy ran to the intersection to help, unaware that the victims in the totaled car were Virginia and me. Dilly and Martin had been at a paramedic conference in Charlotte, North Carolina, the day before and had gotten up early to make the long drive home. They were heading back to Highton via the road Virginia and I usually took to work, and by some odd quirk of fate they drove right up to the wreck barely minutes after it occurred.

Thus it happened that all three men somehow ended up at the scene at the same time—and much sooner than any emergency response team summoned via a 911 phone call.

The bus, incredibly, was undamaged, the children unhurt. The bus had rolled across the hood of the VW, collapsing the passenger compartment, then landed upright in the grass.

Jimmy later admitted to me that none of them could understand how Virginia and I had survived. In fact, the VW was so badly crushed that they were sure anyone in it had been "pancaked"—a crude EMT term for "flattened." Virginia walked away with a minor concussion and lacerated chin; I suffered a fractured wrist. Both of us spent only a single night in the hospital.

Several months after the wreck, Virginia and I were taking a walk during a break at work. We were both silent, enjoying the crisp sunshine, and then suddenly Virginia said, "Kate, can I ask you something about the wreck?"

"Sure," I answered, "what?"

She hesitated. "When we crashed, did you, um, hear a voice and find yourself in some kind of a…a bubble?"

I stopped short and turned to face her. "The voice was male, and he said not to be afraid; that we were going to be all right."

Virginia nodded, not looking at me. "Good. I thought maybe I was crazy."

We never mentioned the subject again.

But to this day I don't doubt there are guardian angels that watch over us. And I'm sure Virginia agrees.

Amanda

Amanda was one of the prettiest girls I'd ever seen. She had long, auburn hair, vivid green eyes, and a sweet smile. I had been called to the junior high school she attended by the school's guidance counselor. Amanda had been a good student, but her grades had begun slipping badly. Once outgoing and friendly, she had become sullen and withdrawn over the last few weeks. She had lost weight, and her mother had pulled her out of the after-school sports she loved.

On the morning when I got the call, Amanda had come to school with a swollen lip. The school nurse determined that one of the wires from her braces had broken and was imbedded in her cheek. Her cheek was as red and swollen as her lip. When the nurse asked her what happened, tears welled in Amanda's eyes and she said softly, "My stepdaddy slapped me."

I sat down with her alone in the guidance counselor's office, introduced myself, and explained why I was there. She was holding an icepack to her face, and she looked at me with frightened eyes.

"I don't want him to get into trouble," she said so quietly I could barely hear her.

I sighed, already suspecting where this was headed. "Sweetheart," I said softly, "I know you don't. But my job is to take care of kids like you—to make sure nobody hurts them. My job is to help your family and to protect you. I don't want to see this happen to you again. I want to help. Will you let me?"

Amanda nodded miserably, more tears welling in her eyes.

It was a long interview. Slowly, and with gentle coaxing on my part, Amanda began to tell her story. Her father had died two years ago. Last summer her mother had married a man she had met at the local evangelical church. He was strict and incredibly abusive: he would make Amanda stand in the corner while her parents ate, and afterward she was given only leftovers. He would tell her that satanic spawn did not deserve to eat. He would beat her with a wooden spoon, telling her it was not him who was beating her, but that the spoon was doing so under the guidance of God. He told her the spankings and hunger would drive the devil out of her. He also began separating her from her friends, forbidding her to participate in intramural sports, school dances, or parties. She had to come straight home after school.

About a month ago he began coming to her room at night. At first he only watched her, but then he began to touch her and force her to touch him.

Tears began spilling down Amanda's cheeks as she spoke. "He told me if I told my mom, he would beat her too. And then..." She stopped and buried her face in her hands. She began to sob.

"Amanda," I said quietly, lifting her chin and looking into her eyes. "There is nothing I haven't heard before. It's okay to tell."

The words came out in a rush. "He t-tried to put it in me. I wouldn't let him. I rolled away from him, but he grabbed me. I screamed, and he slapped me. He called me a l-little whore. Then he locked me in my room and told me I couldn't come out until I learned to obey him. I climbed out the window. I don't know where to g-go," she sobbed. "I don't know where to go."

I sat with her while she cried herself out. Then I gently explained what would happen next.

Amanda revealed that she had told her mother about her stepfather's advances, but her mother had not believed her. In fact, her mother had told her she should go to their church and beg for forgiveness on her knees for making up such lies. Clearly her mother was not going to protect her daughter.

At least Amanda was an only child, which meant I wouldn't need to deal with finding placement for multiple siblings. Foster care in Highton County was hard enough to come by; it was simply impossible to place a sibling group.

Amanda remained in the guidance counselor's office until two special assault detectives arrived from the local sheriff's department. I had already handled several dozen cases with them, and Detectives Bob Morris, Taylor Whit, and I worked well together. When they arrived and set up their paperwork on the guidance counselor's desk, I traded the usual friendly barbs with them, mainly to put Amanda at ease. Then I introduced them to her.

"Bob and Taylor are friends," I told her gently, "and they're here to help. It's okay to talk to them."

Amanda took a deep breath and then bravely and quietly retold her story to the two officers. After she'd finished, they explained that they would be taking her into protective custody, a seventy-two-hour "hold" provided for children during which social workers can place them in foster care until the safety of their home situation can be evaluated. However, before I could take Amanda to her foster home, she would have to undergo a forensic physical examination for rape.

Even though I had talked with her about this, she was understandably terrified as I drove her to the hospital, the detectives following in their car. A pelvic exam can be demeaning for any female. Lying with your feet up in the stirrups, genitalia exposed, and having to tolerate a speculum inserted into your vagina is an uncomfortable procedure at best. For a fourteen-year-old girl undergoing a rape evaluation, it's yet another violation of her body. I held Amanda's hand while she lay mute, eyes closed, tears spilling down her cheeks.

The exam revealed what the doctor and I had expected—nothing. She had resisted her stepfather, and no penetration or ejaculation had occurred.

In most cases of child sexual assault there is little or even no physical evidence—after all, what remains visible when a child is told to fondle an adult?

At this point in my career I had conducted hundreds of child sexual assault interviews. I knew how to differentiate between a truthful disclosure and one that was invented.

A few years later I would become an expert witness on child sexual assault and would teach the courts, counselors, and other social workers the art of disclosure interviewing. Fortunately, the courts generally deemed the child's statements as fact. This resulted in cases like these going against the usual grain of the United States' legal system, where the accused are presumed innocent until proven guilty. In child sexual assault cases, perpetrators are deemed guilty until proven innocent. The reason for this is that the courts consider protecting a child more important than protecting the adult.

But there is one thing that can undo even the most rock-solid assault case: recantation.

Recantation occurs when a child unexpectedly denies the allegation. Recantation is usually prompted by the fact that a child's world is suddenly turned so completely upside down that he or she will do anything—even risk further abuse—to re-right the family and their lives. People often ask me if children lie about being abused. The best response to that question is: Children lie to get out of trouble; they don't lie to get into trouble. And disclosing abuse lands them in a world of trouble.

Living at home in an abusive situation may be horrible, but it is familiar. Being pulled out of their homes, placed in foster care, alienated from their families and friends, being dragged through the family court system, testifying against their own parents, and sometimes losing everything they have can cause even the strongest children to recant.

Alas, Amanda was one of them.

When I went to Amanda's house to interview her mother, she grew livid. She called Amanda a liar and insisted the girl had "made all that up because she's mad at her stepfather for setting limits with her."

Amanda's parents hired a top-notch lawyer and immediately demanded that Amanda take the stand and testify against her parents.

There was nothing I or the detectives could do to prevent that.

The day before the scheduled hearing, Amanda asked if she could visit with her mother and pick up some of her things at her home. I foolishly agreed to allow Amanda this supervised visit. During the visit, Amanda's mother gave her a suitcase filled with her clothing. Stupidly, neither the foster mother nor I thought to look through the case before turning it over to Amanda.

Neither Amanda nor I spoke on the drive back to the foster mother's home. She sat with her arms folded firmly across her chest, and any gentle attempts I made at conversation were rebuffed. I told her I understood how difficult all of this was for her. When we got back to her foster home, I hugged Amanda farewell. Her foster mother, a jewel of a woman, put her arm around Amanda and walked her inside, the suitcase firmly in hand. I watched Amanda lean into her, and I said a quiet prayer of gratitude for the generous family who had taken Amanda in. Nonetheless, I drove home with a feeling of intense unease.

It turned out my worries were justified when the foster mother called me later that night, begging me to come over right away.

When I arrived, Amanda was sitting in the living room crying. She refused to make eye contact with me and ran into her room when I appeared.

"What's going on?" I asked, deeply concerned.

"Take a look at these," the foster mother said.

When I sat down on the sofa, she handed me a stack of letters. There were almost thirty of them. Each one was a handwritten note from a member of the church harshly condemning Amanda for what she had done. Many of the letters contained threats regarding eternal damnation, stating that Amanda would go to hell for disavowing her stepfather, for lying, for whoredom. Her only hope, they had all written, was to admit to her lies and beg forgiveness on her knees from God and the congregation.

I went upstairs to talk with Amanda, but she refused to see me.

At the onset of the hearing the next day, Amanda recanted. She told the judge she had made everything up because she was mad at her stepfather. She had lied, she said, and she was ever so sorry for what she had done to hurt her mother, her stepfather, and the members of her church.

The judge ordered her back home and closed the case. When her stepfather got up and attempted to hug her, Amanda stood there white-faced, arms hanging rigidly at her sides.

As the family filed out of the courtroom, I managed to exchange a few private words with her.

"Amanda," I said softly, "you know how to reach me. I will always be here for you. If you want help, day or night, call me. Please."

Amanda's eyes filled with tears as she looked up into mine. "Not even God can help me now," she whispered.

Of Props and Teddy Bears

I returned from court to my office one afternoon to find an elderly woman waiting for me. An adorable four-year-old girl with blond hair and huge blue eyes was playing at her feet, but she popped her thumb in her mouth and scooted fearfully toward the woman, her grandmother, as I approached.

I shook hands with the grandmother and then crouched down beside the child. "Hi, Bettina," I said with a smile. "I'm Kate. It's nice to meet you."

Bettina clutched a ragged teddy bear to her and stared at me with solemn eyes. I had already read the intake report before I left for court earlier that morning. The grandmother had been caring for Bettina in her home while her parents worked.

Yesterday morning she had gone to pick up Bettina as usual, only to find that the little girl was still in her pajamas and that her hair was smeared with what looked—and smelled—like semen. When she confronted her daughter and son-in-law, they had told her to mind her own business.

Disgusted, the grandmother had grabbed Bettina and fled the house. Unfortunately, she had given Bettina a bath and washed her hair and clothing before realizing that perhaps she should have saved the semen-stained pajamas as evidence. She had taken the child to the pediatrician, who found no evidence of abuse, but Bettina told the doctor that her daddy had "rubbed on me and icky white stuff came out." The doctor had promptly called us.

I now placed a call to Bob Morris at Special Assault, and he came to the office immediately. He watched from behind a two-way mirror as I sat down on the floor with Bettina and began coloring with her. Child sexual assault interviewing is tricky and requires a great deal of patience. It is critical to ask only open-ended questions and to never lead the child. I often used stuffed animals, huge sheets of coloring paper, crayons, and other toys to help children describe what happened to them.

Bettina and I decided we would play house with several dolls. On a large sheet of poster paper we drew Bettina's room—she showed me where her bed and dresser were, and where she kept her clothes and dolls. Her favorite toy was her stuffed bear, Brownie. She showed me how she and Brownie slept in her bed and her other dolls in a toy box, which she had me draw at the foot of her "bed."

I asked her where her mommy and daddy slept, and she had me draw a room next to hers.

"But sometimes," she said without prompting, "the daddy doll comes and sleeps with the baby."

I picked up the little girl doll and placed it on the drawing of the parents' bed.

Bettina giggled and said, "No, dummy! Here!" She pointed to the drawing of her own bed.

"Can you show me where the daddy doll and the baby doll sleep?" I asked.

Bettina pushed the two dolls onto her "bed."

"Then what?" I asked.

"Then," she said firmly, "they play tickle! Only don't tell, don't tell, or Daddy will get mad."

"Don't tell what?" I asked nonchalantly.

Bettina grabbed the daddy doll and rubbed its crotch against the baby doll's face.

"Bettina," I said softly and still very calmly, "has anyone ever done that to you?"

Bettina looked up at me. "Uh-huh. Daddy. And then icky white stuff comes out. I'm not supposed to tell." She turned back to the baby doll. "Don't tell!" she scolded the doll. "Don't tell, or Mommy will get really, really mad."

***

Bob Morris took Bettina into protective custody, and I placed her in the grandmother's care. I then paid a visit to the parents' home. Bettina's mother was home alone when I showed up, and she angrily denied the allegations.

"She's only four years old," she snorted. "What an imagination! She has such a huge imagination. She walked in on my husband and me having sex once; I'm sure that's where she got this from."

I asked her about the semen on Bettina's hair and pajamas. "How can my mother say such a thing? That's disgusting! It was just glue—we were doing an art project, and she smeared glue in her hair."

I sighed. Obviously this case was going to court.

Child sexual assault cases are handled in one of two kinds of trials. The first is a family court hearing in which the safety of the child is assessed and the court determines whether or not the seventy-two-hour protective custody hold is warranted. The second is a criminal court trial held to determine the guilt or innocence of the alleged perpetrator.

The vast majority of child sexual offenders, or pedophiles, are well known to the child. Mothers' boyfriends and stepfathers unfortunately vie for first place in this category (women very rarely sexually abuse children). Pedophiles work hard at earning a child's trust, and thus many offenders are well known, often loved, and viewed as respected members of their community. This is one of the reasons that disbelief is usually the first response by others toward an allegation of abuse against an individual.

When an allegation of abuse is made, the immediate protection of the child comes first. Criminal prosecution is secondary. Once the allegation is investigated and a social intake worker finds it is most likely true, then the safety of the child is assessed.

If the child's mother or other guardian does not appear willing or able to protect the child from the perpetrator, then the child is placed either in foster care or, preferably, with a protective family member. The social worker then requests a series of intervention services, which usually include a sexual deviancy evaluation of the offending parent, a psychological evaluation of the mother, counseling, and any other supportive services that will hopefully help to reunite the family while protecting the child.

Unfortunately, there is no "cure" for pedophilia, the sexual attraction to children. The goal is to ensure the mother's protectiveness of her child. Marriages usually break up over these events. In rarer cases, the mothers end up siding with their husbands or, more commonly, their boyfriends, and turn their backs on their children.

Unfortunately, Bettina's mother was this type of parent. She never wavered from her belief that Bettina was lying. Bob Morris filed criminal charges of indecent liberties against Bettina's father, and he pleaded not guilty.

The result of all this was that the case had to go to trial. This also meant that four-year-old Bettina was going to have to testify against her parents.

Preparing a child for court is never easy. The first thing I usually do is take the child and her support person, in this case Bettina's grandmother, into an empty courtroom. We tour the room, let the child sit on the witness stand and on the judge's bench, and perform a brief mock-up of a hearing. This way the child hopefully understands a little about what to expect during the trial and not be afraid of the setting or the strangers involved.

Fortunately, at the initial hearing phase and in all family court matters, there are no juries—only the judge, the court reporter, a bailiff, the defendants, and the child. Because Bettina's initial hearing fell under the jurisdiction of the family court, it would be closed. Needless to say, I hated putting children through this traumatic experience, but often there was no other option.

The morning of Bettina's hearing dawned sunny and hot. Bettina and her grandmother arrived at court early. Bettina was wearing a pretty yellow sundress and was, as usual, clutching Brownie Bear.

I hurried Bettina and her grandmother into the courtroom before her parents arrived then sat down at the table with the CPS family court attorney, Patrick Brower, and Detective Bob Morris. Earlier I had shifted the defense table off to the side so that Bettina would be looking straight at her grandmother and me, not at her parents. And luckily this was not Judge John Dawley's court.

Bettina's mother and father entered with their attorney. I watched to see what Bettina's mother's reaction would be at seeing her daughter. I prayed she would burst into tears and hug the little girl to her. My heart sank as she glared at her instead.

Bettina's grandmother held the little girl's hand as we rose for the judge's entrance then took our seats.

Bettina's parents' attorney stood up. "I would like to ask to approach the bench without my clients or the child and her grandmother present."

The judge looked at me and the two attorneys sitting with me, and we nodded our consent. My heart rose. Perhaps Bettina's parents had changed their minds and would plead guilty, sparing their daughter the need to testify.

Bettina, her grandmother, and the parents left the room. I asked the bailiff to please make sure they were kept separated in order to prevent Bettina's parents from saying anything to her that might cause the little girl not to testify if the need for that arose, which I now hoped it wouldn't. The bailiff was familiar with CPS cases, and he immediately steered the parents into a separate waiting room.

Watching them leave, I breathed a sigh of relief.

When the courtroom was empty save for Detective Morris, the attorneys, the judge, and me, the parents' attorney began.

"Your Honor!" he bellowed without warning. "I am voicing a protest! This child has been clearly prompted as to what to say. Furthermore, she has been cleverly dressed to look innocent. I'm sure," he sneered, turning to address me, "you spent a great deal of time choosing that cute little dress."

Shock and anger welled in my gut, but I knew to bite my feelings back and keep my expression impassive.

"And," the attorney continued, re-directing his attention to the judge, "my clients are requesting that the grandmother be barred from the room during the proceedings."

I gasped. This sleaze-ball attorney was doing his best to make the upcoming testimony as frightening and difficult for Bettina as possible. It took every ounce of self-control for me not to open my mouth and let the attorney have a double-barrel barrage of verbal assault. Goading social workers into anger is one of their most tried and true ploys, a method in which defense attorneys try to show prejudice on the social worker's part. I had fallen into that trap once and had sworn never to do it again.

It had happened with a case similar to Bettina's—a mother who refused to believe her children's allegations that her boyfriend was molesting them. She would leave her daughters, five and seven years old, alone with him again and again. By the time the case came to the attention of Child Protective Services, the girls had been raped repeatedly. The perpetrator's defense attorney launched into a tirade in court that it was my fault as the CPS social worker for not having intervened sooner and that I had exaggerated the allegations because I was prejudiced toward the father, who was not born in America. He then implied that I specialized in sexual assault cases because it was titillating to me.

At that point I blew up and shouted at the attorney, "You are as big a slime as your client!"

The attorney of course had a field day with that, telling the judge it was clear that I was indeed prejudiced toward his client—I had, after all, just referred to him as "slime" in court. The focus in the case was thus shifted to me and my ability to perform an unbiased investigation.

As a result, the case was deferred and re-investigated, which meant that the poor girls ended up having to remain in foster care longer and undergo another forensic physical examination. There was no getting around the fact that my angry outburst had caused further pain for two innocent children, and I swore from that day on that no matter how angry I became, I would bite it back, ignore the assault, and remain impassive. I can't even pretend that it was easy. Remaining quiet and calm, especially in Judge John Dawley's court, often took every bit of self-control I could muster, and then some. But it helped to remind myself of those two little girls to find the self-control I so often desperately needed.

Now I assumed this practiced demeanor while Bettina's attorney ranted on and on. Inside, however, I was so furious that I was shaking. The attorney, meanwhile, strutted dramatically around the room and stopped directly in front of the judge. He leaned toward the bench and lowered his voice to a conspiratorial whisper.

"…In addition to that, the child has been given a prop. A prop, Your Honor." He paused for dramatic emphasis. "I demand that this prop—the teddy bear—be barred from this courtroom as well."

I uttered a strangled gasp. The slimy piece of shit! I wanted to leap to my feet and roar out a protest. Patrick, my attorney, must have sensed the rage welling in me, because he quietly put his hand on my shoulder.

Judge Howard Foster leaned back in his chair and closed his eyes for a moment. I thought I saw his jaw clench. Was it my imagination or was he too fighting to keep his anger under control?

When he opened his eyes, he glared down at the parents' attorney. "Counselor," he said coldly, "this is a closed CPS hearing. As such, unfortunately, I have to abide by your request that the grandmother, as a non-party to this case, be barred from this courtroom."

My heart sank. My rage grew.

He continued, "I'm not sure what the hell you meant with that comment about the little girl's dress, and I'm not even going to grace that with my attention."

There was a moment of silence before he shook his head in what I could only hope was disgust.

"As for the teddy bear…" Judge Foster leaned forward. "I'm barring the grandmother because I have to. But don't push me, Counselor. Don't push me. The bear stays."

A dizzying wave of relief washed over me.

The opposing attorney was smart enough to shut his mouth, look contrite, and sit back down. I again felt the gentle pressure of a hand on my shoulder—Bob Morris's this time. I let out my breath. I hadn't realized I'd been holding it.

When I went to fetch Bettina, I asked her if she would be all right without her grandmother. She nodded uncertainly.

"I'll be right by you, Bettina," I told her. "And just as soon as you tell Judge Foster the truth, I'll bring you back to your grandmother, okay?"

Bettina nodded again, looking relieved.

"Okay, we're going to go back into the courtroom now. Just remember, Bettina, you have to tell the truth, right?"

Bettina nodded solemnly. "Right!" Clutching her bear, she marched into the courtroom as resolutely as a four-year-old could.

***

It would be another thirty years before a Seattle, Washington, therapist created the nonprofit Courthouse Dogs Foundation and the "Courthouse Dog" program. The premise of this program is that children who have to testify in a court of law gain courage and are comforted when they are permitted to have a facility dog—a service dog assigned to an institution rather than an individual—sitting in the courtroom with them.

Some children pet the dog, which is trained to unobtrusively interact with them, while others testify with their arms firmly wrapped around the dog's neck. The dog offers them an outlet for their fears, a sense of security, and a place to look when they cannot meet a perpetrator's eye. Defense attorneys fought the program when it was first launched, but it soon gained widespread acceptance. As of this writing, there are hundreds of trained facility dogs working throughout the United States.

Unfortunately for Bettina, this program was not yet in place when she was asked to testify against her parents. As I escorted her into the courtroom, I worried that she would become frightened and be unable—or unwilling—to speak.

But my worry was for naught. The defense attorney must have read more in Judge Foster's look than that scolding over a yellow dress and a brown teddy bear, because the man spoke gently and kindly to the little girl. He asked her only two questions—to identify the people in the room ("Mommy and Daddy," she answered) and if she could tell us why she was here. ("Because Daddy rubbed his pee-pee on me and yucky stuff came out.")

When it was Patrick's turn to speak, he praised her for her bravery and asked if she had told her mother about this. "Daddy told me not to tell," she answered. "But I told her!" She pointed at me. "And I told my grandma."

Then she looked up at her father and mother. Tears welled in her eyes. "I'm sorry, Daddy, I'm sorry!" she sobbed.

The judge immediately motioned for me to take Bettina from the courtroom. When we reached the hall, I sank to my knees and held her tight. I could not fight back my own tears. "You were so brave," I whispered, "you were so, so brave!"

***

Six months later the case went into severance of parental rights. I made one final visit to Bettina's mother. The most pressing question I asked her was why she had chosen Bettina's father over her daughter. I was not yet a mother myself, but I still couldn't fathom how a mother could abandon her own child. Bettina's mother was making exactly this choice.

She looked at me without expression. "In fourteen years my daughter will be grown and out of the house. I will be alone. But my husband will be with me for the rest of my life."

I thought about that comment years later when I held my newborn daughter in my arms. As I gazed into her perfect little face, I understood even less how a mother could ever choose to let her own child go. And I wondered often if Bettina's mother ever regretted her choice.

"Take Them, They're Yours."

I arrived at the office early one morning to find our secretary sitting on the front steps with two small children. She was holding the infant, a chubby-cheeked little boy dressed in a sailor suit. A little girl, perhaps three years old, was sitting beside her. She too was dressed in a blue sailor suit. The kids were adorable, and I grinned at Deanne as I approached.

"Bring your grandkids to work day?" I guessed.

Deanne shook her head no and handed me an envelope. I sat down beside her, pulled the three-year-old onto my lap, and opened the envelope.

The neat lettering said simply, *I can't handle them anymore. Take them. They're yours.*

"They were sitting here when I drove up this morning," Deanne told me. "This is Nicole," she said, tousling the curls of the little girl sitting on my lap, "and Nicole tells me this is her brother, Liam. Nicole doesn't know her last name, address, or phone number," Deanne added.

I closed my eyes and sighed. This was a case for permanency planning, not my unit. Two children dumped on a doorstep like a litter of unwanted kittens. Well, at least the mother had brought them to a safe place. (The creation of "Safe Place," a national program that provides facilities where overwhelmed parents can drop off their children, was still over twenty years in the future.)

"Is Mommy coming soon?" Nicole asked me. My heart sank. How could I answer that? These were not the first children left at our office, and they wouldn't be the last. In most of these cases the children were left by single mothers who had simply reached the end of their rope. Most any parent working outside of the home can relate how difficult it is to juggle a job, child-rearing, and housework. Now couple those challenges with a minimum-wage job, a completely absent father who fails to pay any child support, and a lack of familial or community help, programs, or safety nets. It's no wonder some of these moms simply give up.

Contrary to social myth, few of these mothers are drug addicted or abandon their children so they can pursue a relationship with a new boyfriend. Even less are involved in prostitution or other illegal activities. Many are depressed but cannot afford therapy or anti-depressant medication. Fortunately for many of these families, once social service interventions—childcare, food stamps, home-help, and AFDC—are put into place, the family is usually able to be reunited and supported. I prayed this would end up as one of those cases.

But if not, where would these two precious children go? Finding competent parents to foster children is one of the most difficult tasks social workers face. I often wished that biological parents had to undergo even half the evaluations that foster parents did. Health and physical fitness, intelligence testing, psychological evaluations, home safety—you name it, they were screened for it. They were required to take parenting classes, first aid, and CPR; they had to attend training classes and ongoing foster parent meetings, not to mention being called in to hearings, asked to testify in court, haul children to medical, dental, or mental health appointments…the list was endless. And most of them did it with incredibly good humor.

I had long since come to respect foster parents as the true salt of the earth. These selfless individuals took in the world's unwanted, unloved, and mistreated children. Raising kids is tough—now compound the usual challenges of parenthood with a child who is not yours, comes with mental health issues, physical issues, fear issues; a child who may have been sodomized or raped by his or her parents; a child who may have faced every single day of life without love or nurturing.

I've heard comments that foster parents "do it for the money." In truth the reimbursement for these kids is so pitiful that it hardly begins to touch the expenses many of these parents incur. When asked why they do it, invariably the foster parents will smile and say "out of love, of course," and I for one believe them.

Desperate to recruit more foster parents, my supervisor had long ago arranged for me to speak on a regular basis at area community functions, and I did so gladly. One such function had been with a group of anti-abortion advocates who met regularly at a local church to knit baby booties and receiving blankets for charity. I always followed a routine during these presentations that included showing slides with statistics about child abuse and neglect, local intake and case numbers, and facts about child protective services. I also talked about the scope of abuse and neglect and who the average perpetrators were.

When I finished this particular presentation a woman stood up. "I don't believe you," she said sharply. "I think you're making this up. I'm not sure what your motive is, but it's disgusting. You should be ashamed of yourself."

Taken aback, I wasn't sure how to respond. "Why do you think I'm making this up?" I finally asked her.

"Nobody treats a child that way! All children are wanted. I'm proud to say we ladies here are always able to find homes for every baby born in this area."

The other women nodded vigorously.

"Thank you for what you do," I said sincerely, "but I wish I could agree with you that every child is wanted. The truth is that far too many are not."

She gestured contemptuously at the slide projector. "And I still say you're making all of that up."

Taking a deep breath, I told them calmly about a newborn boy recently found alive in a dumpster and another left in a paper bag in a restroom trash can. Both stories had made national headlines. I told them about a pretty young girl I had visited in a group home (some people refer to them as "orphanages") just a few days ago. She was sixteen and had spent her life from age five until now living in various group homes. She told me that she had come to the realization that no one had ever wanted her and that no one ever would.

"Well then, there must have been something wrong with her!" the woman snapped, ignoring my reference to the abandoned newborns altogether. Again the others nodded their agreement.

"If being born to parents who don't want you makes you 'wrong,' then I guess you could call this girl and all the others like her 'wrong.' It's easy to place Caucasian newborn babies like the newborn found in the dumpster," I explained. "It's almost impossible to place older children, non-white children, sibling groups, or children with physical or mental handicaps."

"Not true!" the woman shouted at me.

I kept my voice calm and gentle. "I know this is hard to accept. But the truth is, people don't want these children. They are 'damaged goods.' And that's why I'm here—to ask if any of you would consider becoming foster parents. Please. We need you."

I wish I could say that I recruited a whole bunch of new foster parents that evening, but the reality was that not one single person stepped forward. Not one. And I found the same to be true of similar groups I spoke to. These people advocated for the right of all children to be born, but beyond buying cribs and clothing and knitting booties for pregnant women who did not want their babies, they did nothing to care for the children once they were born. Maybe they believed that some sort of "mothering instinct" kicked in at birth and that the baby would then be wanted, loved, and cared for. I was appalled at their blindness.

Now I lifted Nicole into my arms. "Come on," I said as encouragingly as I could, "let's see what we can find for breakfast." Walking into the office with Nicole's chubby little arms around my neck, I wondered, not for the last time, when the very opinionated people I spoke to might open their eyes, minds, hearts, and especially their homes, to children like her.

Held at Gunpoint

Nick and Lauren Wainwright were, from all appearances, the perfect couple. His father owned a chain of grocery stores where Nick was employed. Lauren was an elementary schoolteacher. The couple was active in the local church, and they had two beautiful children, aged three and seven. Nick was about as nice and polite a young man as anyone could hope to meet. He was a devoted husband and a great daddy—until he got drunk. When Nick Wainwright drank, he got mean. Real mean.

I first encountered the family when I responded to their home as an EMT. Nick had beaten Lauren almost senseless. When she came to in the hospital, she denied that he had hit her. The next morning a contrite Nick appeared at the hospital, bringing his wife flowers and showering her with kisses and apologies. He called himself a heel, a drunk, a cad, and he promised never, ever to so much as raise his voice toward her again. He swore he was giving up the bottle. Lauren fell in love all over again, smothered him with kisses, and the cycle of abuse continued.

This was prior to the days when abusive spouses could be arrested without statement from their partners, and although as a CPS social worker I desperately wanted to remove the children from this unstable, volatile home, I didn't have the power to do so. Back then physical evidence of abuse was needed before CPS could intervene—risk was not enough.

But Nick Wainwright was smart even when he was drunk. He loved his kids and was careful to never, ever harm them. Until one night when he was beating Lauren with a belt. The oldest boy grabbed his mother around the waist and yelled at his daddy to leave her alone. Nick swung the belt anyway, aiming the buckle at Lauren. He missed, and the belt caught the little boy across the cheek. We had a mark. Lauren was hospitalized, and Bob Morris and I placed the children in protective custody and foster care. Nick fled.

It was after midnight before I returned home from placing the Wainwright children that day. I fell into bed exhausted, and as a result I overslept and arrived at the office nearly an hour late. The parking lot was full and no one was about. Everyone was already inside, working. I got out of my car and headed to the DSHS employee entrance only to find Nick Wainwright standing by the door. As soon as he saw me he walked toward me and stopped right in front of me.

"Where are my kids?" he demanded.

I drew in a deep breath. "Hey, Nick. They're safe. Why don't you come inside and let's talk?"

Nick was wearing a jacket in spite of the hot day, and now he partially lifted something out of his pocket. It was a gun.

"No, how about you and me get in your car. You drive."

I swallowed hard, but I knew better than to argue with a man holding a gun. I started walking back to my car, praying that one of my co-workers happened to be looking out of the window. Even so, I knew I had only one chance with Nick. Unarmed and at his mercy, my only weapon was my head—and my heart. I prayed that I would say the right things.

The car was parked about twenty feet from the building. As I got in and started to pull the door shut, Deanne, the office secretary, appeared from around the corner. Nick froze, hands in his pockets. "Mornin', Kate!" Deanne said cheerfully as she walked by.

I looked up and caught her eye. "Good morning," I answered back and then mouthed, "Help me!" I prayed she would see and Nick wouldn't. But Deanne just waved and turned back toward the building, and my heart plummeted as she disappeared inside.

Nick immediately got into the passenger side of my car, slamming the door behind him. "Where are my fucking kids?" he demanded.

I took a deep breath. "Nick, I'm sorry about your kids. My job is to—"

"Where are my fucking kids?" he repeated.

I breathed deeply again. "The police took them into protective custody last night. They're in a temporary foster home until we can get you and Lauren straightened out. Will you let me help?"

"Shit." Nick slammed his fist on the dashboard.

"Nick, I really want to help." I spoke quietly and clearly, letting him know I cared, reassuring him that I wanted to help, that I wanted him and Lauren to make it work and get their children back as soon as possible.

Nick sat back and listened as I talked. When I fell silent he began to talk, telling me about how his father was a mean drunk and that he'd sworn never to be like him. As he revealed all this to me I glanced in the rearview mirror. My heart stopped when I saw police cars pouring into the DSHS parking lot. Their doors burst open as I watched and officers raced out and surrounded the building with guns drawn. That would have been fine, except that I was outside of that protective ring, in a car behind them. I wanted to scream. How could they be so stupid?

I looked up and could see one of my co-workers in the window. She was gesturing wildly toward my car and mouthing the words, "They're in the car! They're in the car!"

Nick looked up at that moment. "Shit! Are they here for me?"

I drew in another breath. "Yeah, they are."

"Shit! Put this thing in gear and get out of here!" he barked.

"Nick," I said quietly, my heart pounding, "we have some choices here. If we take off, chances are they're going to open fire and you, and probably me too, are going to get killed. Or you can get out of the car, and they'll most likely gun you down. Or we can both get out of this car together, safely, and I swear to you, Nick, I will do everything I can to help you fix this mess and get your family back."

By now the police had realized their mistake and were surrounding the car, guns pointed at us. I was terrified they'd open fire.

Nick hesitated and looked at me pleadingly. Finally he nodded. He pulled a toy gun out of his pocket and handed it to me. I prayed the officers weren't trigger-happy as Nick and I slowly stepped out of the car together, Nick with his hands in the air.

The officers immediately jumped him and threw him to the ground. It was Bob Morris who grabbed me.

"Kate, you all right?"

I slumped against him. "I'm...I'm fine," I stammered. My knees felt like putty. My stomach roiled. I grinned weakly at him. "Well, maybe, I, um, I just need to go home and change my pants."

Nick Wainwright was sentenced to a year in prison. During that time Lauren divorced him and remarried quickly. I saw her again about two years later when we happened to run into each other at a local state park. She seemed happy and was clearly expecting another baby. Nick was out of jail, she told me, and had been clean and sober ever since his arrest. He had regained visitation rights with the children and was, in Lauren's words, "a good daddy."

She walked away smiling. I couldn't help but smile too. Maybe Maryann Tevis was right. Sometimes things did work out.

Of Arsenic and Quilts

The school nurse alerted us to a family of five children living in a trailer with their parents. The children showed all the typical signs of neglect: they were dirty, smelly, and behind in their schooling even though they were clearly intelligent. The school nurse had received a shock one morning when she made a home visit to talk with the children's mother about their school-required immunizations.

"Oh, they don't need 'em," the mother had responded dismissively. "Them kids ain't never gonna get sick. I give 'em a pinch of arsenic a week. That keeps 'em healthier than any of them shots you want to give."

Horrified, the nurse had called us. Blood work revealed that the children were indeed being fed arsenic—an old mountain remedy that supposedly warded off illness.

After an extensive interview, I determined that ignorance was to blame and that the parents were at least marginally protective of their children. After a lengthy case staffing and court appearance, it was decided that the children could remain at home but that a slew of intervention services would be offered to the family. The mother, Amy, sullenly agreed, but the father remained withdrawn, angry, and resistive.

Visiting the family at home was a challenge in many ways. On my second home visit, while I was trying to keep my Toyota from veering off the rutted dirt road, I swerved to miss a rock that would have meant the end of my oil pan and ran over a chicken. Knowing that poultry was often a mountain family's primary food source, I immediately submitted a requisition for a new chicken.

My supervisor, Hilary, eyed the request and grumbled, "Why don't you just bring them a bucket of Kentucky Fried and call it even?"

The next time I visited the family, I appeared with both a check and a young chicken in a box. Amy took the box without comment, but she refused the check. "Bird waren't worth that much," she explained.

I quickly learned that whenever I knocked on the trailer it was best to stand aside. That's because when the door opened, I never knew whether a blast of chaw, spit, or the barrel of a shotgun would be aimed at me. It all depended on who was home and what kind of mood they were in.

Whenever I went inside, Amy (who was usually the only one there) and I would sit in silence. She seemed unable—or unwilling—to work with me, and I was at my wit's end about how to reach her. The answer came during a Christmas visit to my parents' home. My brothers and sister were all home as well, and I was sitting on the sofa bouncing my fourteen-month-old nephew on my knee. He was giggling.

What a contrast to the families I worked with, I thought. Here was a little boy born into a secure, peaceful home with parents who were well-educated, nurturing, and who doted on him. His future was bright and secure. There was no doubt that he was loved and would be a loving adult in turn.

I sat bolt upright. That was it! That was the answer! My clients were unable to nurture their children because they themselves had never been nurtured! What if...what if I could find a way to nurture these parents and teach them how in turn to nurture their children through experience?

But how did one nurture an adult?

I posed the question to my colleagues as soon as I got back to work. Most of our clients were too poor to take care of themselves, let alone their children. Haircuts, cosmetics, dentistry, new clothes, and pretty things with which to decorate their homes were far beyond the financial means of almost all of them.

"How about," I suggested, "if I start out with simple meetings in which these moms can be nurtured? Say, get their hair cut and styled, give them manicures, get them some nice clothes. Maybe cleaning up the house isn't the answer; maybe we can make them want to do it themselves by somehow making their homes something they can be proud of?"

Hilary sighed. "I don't put much faith in this, Kate, but go ahead, give it a try. Only there isn't any money in the budget for this type of stuff."

I began by making a lot of phone calls. I asked a local beauty shop what they would charge for cutting and styling some CPS clients' hair.

The proprietress said, "I have a better idea. Why don't you call a beauty college? There may be one in Madison, and I'm pretty sure there's one in Asheville. I bet one of them can help you."

I phoned up the director of the nearest school, a sharp, energetic woman named Nora. She listened to my proposal.

"Tell you what," she said. "How about we bring the school to your clients? You just need to find us a place to meet. We can set up portable washbasins, hairdryers, and all the rest. It will be part of our students' education. No charge."

Excited, I telephoned a local church. The secretary promptly offered us the use of the church's large basement for free.

Next I invited my clients. To my surprise, six of the mothers agreed. Since none of them drove, the home-help worker and I picked them up in our cars and brought them to the church where the beauty school students were waiting.

The next two hours were spent in a whirlwind of activity. The women had their hair washed and cut by the stylists, they waxed their brows, and showed them how to apply makeup. They gave each woman a comb and brush, makeup samples, and, depending on whether or not they had electricity in the home, curlers or a blow dryer. They showed them how to style their own hair and promised they would be back in two months.

As they were packing up to leave, I thanked Nora profusely. "My pleasure!" She grinned. "This was worth it."

I asked each of the women if they were willing to meet again the following week.

"What are we gonna do?" they wanted to know.

I had already thought of that and had made the appropriate plans. A local florist had invited us in to show them how to do flower arranging—again at no charge.

To my delight, they all agreed.

After the class, which turned out to be a great success with all the women making their own arrangements and getting to take them home, I drove one of the mothers, a woman named Lillian, back to her house.

Lillian's home was filthy. I knew, because I'd already been inside a number of times. The home-help specialist had tried for weeks to work with her, but Lillian had remained resistive. She didn't seem to care that she and her children stank, that her dogs left feces on the floor, or that she stored coal in her bathtub. But she had agreed to come to what I was now inwardly referring to as my "parenting classes."

On the drive home, Lillian proudly held her creation on her lap. Now, as we stepped into her kitchen, we both stopped and looked around. We both realized that there was no place to put the flower arrangement amid the stacks of dirty dishes, rotting food, piles of old newspapers, garbage, Crisco cans, and empty bottles.

"Hang on to this," Lillian said. She handed the arrangement to me. Next she gathered up the dishes on the kitchen table and carried them to the sink. She grabbed a rag and wiped down the kitchen table, then set the flowers on it.

She eyed the result. "Don't look too good, does it?"

"It, um, kind of gets lost in the clutter," I agreed.

Lillian looked at me. "Recon that home-help lady you wanted me to work with might help me clean up a little?"

I grinned. "I know she would!"

When I got back to the office I told Sarah what had happened. She grinned as widely as I had earlier and headed straight out to her car.

I heard nothing at all from Sarah for the rest of the day. It was dark when I left the office. Just as I was getting into my car, Sarah pulled up.

"How'd it go?" I asked as she opened the door and got out.

If possible, she was smiling even more broadly than when she'd driven away hours before.

"You will not believe it, Kate! We cleaned up that damned kitchen. In fact, we scrubbed it till it shone."

"Really?"

Sarah nodded excitedly. "In fact, I'm going back tomorrow with a trailer—there are about thirty sacks of garbage to go to the dump. When we were done, Lillian said, 'The rest of the house don't look too good neither, does it?'"

By now Sarah was laughing. "I've got my work cut out for me this week."

***

I returned to Lillian's house a few days later. I could not believe I was in the same place. Sarah had arranged for a local scout troop to clean out, mow, and weed Lillian's yard. Inside, the house was immaculate. It was still old and worn, but the floors and counters were clean and sparkling; clothes were hanging in the closets; and, most surprising of all, the coal was gone from the bathtub.

Sarah showed me where the scout troop had built a coal bin in a shed in the yard. She had purchased soap and shampoo and had told Lillian that since her hair looked so nice now, she might want to show it off by keeping it clean and brushed.

The biggest change was Lillian herself. She was clean and had exchanged the yellowed shift she always wore for a nice pair of slacks and a blouse. Admittedly she had on too much of the makeup given to her by the beauty school, but to me she was beautiful.

"It looks nice in here, don't it?" she said proudly.

"Yes, it really does. And so do you!"

Lillian beamed.

Sarah continued weekly home visits with Lillian. She encouraged Lillian to send the kids to school regularly, helped enroll her in a women's group at church, and even after I closed out her case, Lillian asked if she could keep coming to the weekly parenting meetings.

I agreed.

By now the meetings had grown from six women to over a dozen. Most showed up willingly as word got out; only a few still had to be forced to attend on court order.

One of these mothers, Amy, had to be picked up and brought to the meetings by the sheriff. Angry, she sat in the back of the room, arms folded, refusing to participate.

We spent our meetings doing crafts or other projects and brought in guest speakers that included self-help experts, motivational speakers, artists and craftsmen, and even a dentist. We took trips to a local zoo and visited gardens; on one occasion a culinary institute provided a gourmet catered dinner at no cost.

Once the women were comfortable with the meeting procedure and each other, I gradually introduced group counseling, and the women began to share their frustrations and feelings with each other. They asked to meet twice a week. I sent in a proposal for funding to the state Department of Social and Health Services. I was awarded a $3,000 grant for continuing the sessions.

***

One wet morning I asked the group, now grown to over twenty women, what they might like to do the following week. Did anyone have a talent they wanted to share? Until this point Amy had been attending because she was court ordered to, but she had still refused to participate and remained sullen and angry. Now, to my utmost surprise, Amy spoke up.

"I can quilt," she said.

"You can what?"

"Quilt," she answered. "I can teach the group to quilt."

The next day Sarah and I went to Amy's home. For the first time ever she willingly invited us in. Neatly folded on the living room floor was a stack of quilts. They were spectacular. Flowers, chevrons, diamonds of every color imaginable spilled out of the pile.

"Amy, may I buy one of these?" Sarah asked.

"Why sure! What you think they're worth? Ten dollars?"

Sarah gasped. "Amy, you could sell these for ten times that at any art fair!"

Amy looked stunned. "A hundred dollars? Who'd pay a hundred dollars for a quilt?"

"City people," Sarah answered, holding up a beautiful creation of roses and sunflowers. "City people who love and appreciate mountain art."

Sarah and I used some of the grant money to purchase bolts of fabric, batting, needles, thread, and scissors from a local millinery store. We arranged for a lumber company to donate material to build quilting racks.

Soon Amy was guiding the group through the making of appliqué quilts, pillows, and purses.

Sarah arranged for Amy to sell her quilts at local art fairs and galleries. The response was more than gratifying. Best of all, Amy found a job at a local sewing notions store.

A few months after offering to teach the group quilting, Amy spoke up for the first time during the group's counseling session. She stated without hesitating that she had kicked out her husband. "He was a lazy good-for-nothin'," she told us, and revealed that he frequently beat her and the kids when he was drunk. Finally, when he had tried to "have his way" with their oldest daughter, Amy had threatened him with a butcher knife and kicked him out. Now that she was earning her own money she no longer needed him.

As Amy talked, I studied her face. It was open and smiling. What a huge difference from the sullen, angry woman I had first met. Once again I thought of Maryann Tevis and how right she had been.

Of Angels and Bicycles

It was Christmas Eve. I was alone in the office, working late. Everyone else had left over an hour ago to begin their holiday festivities. This was the first Christmas I would be spending without my family since I had to be back at work the day after Christmas, which didn't leave enough time for travelling to Connecticut.

I was miserable. Peter and I had been fighting lately; the pressure of my job was taking its toll on both of us. We had planned on taking the afternoon off to be together, but at the last minute he had been called into the office, so I thought, *what the heck. I'll just work late too.*

I was tired. The other social workers and I had spent the month before the holidays buying, begging, creating, bargaining—anything and everything we could think of to obtain Christmas food, trees, and gifts for our clients. Between the generosity of several churches and other charities, we were able to scrape together everything on the wish lists we had received from the parents and children who made up our caseloads.

Except for one thing: a white banana-seat bicycle. They were all the rage that year. A ten-year-old boy on my caseload had asked for nothing but a white banana-seat bicycle.

I had done everything I could to find him one. I had called bike shops for miles around; I had hunted through toy stores and second-hand shops, checked newspaper ads and went to garage sales to no avail.

Now it was six o'clock, well past time to go home. It was dark and snowing, and I wasn't feeling in a Christmas mood. In fact, I felt more like Ebenezer Scrooge.

Earlier in the day I had approached the man selling Christmas trees in the parking lot near our office and asked if he was willing to donate a tree for one of our clients. He had refused, which, granted, I couldn't fault him for as I knew there was usually a last-minute rush for trees and he no doubt had his own family to feed. At four thirty everyone had cleared the office and gone home—except me. But now that it was dark and the roads were already powdered with snow, I decided to pack up and leave.

As I switched off the office light I heard a knock on the outer door. I unlocked it and found the Christmas tree guy standing there. He had lined a dozen trees against our office wall.

"Here are the trees you wanted."

I smiled apologetically. "Thanks, but we can't use them now. There's no one here to distribute them."

"Too bad, lady, 'cause they're your problem now."

"Hey!" I shouted as he turned to go. "You can't just dump your unsold trees on us!"

He turned and actually sneered at me. "You asked for 'em; you got 'em!" With that he turned and vanished into the swirling white darkness.

Great, I fumed. Now it would be our responsibility to haul off his stupid trees. What a jerk!

I called the sheriff's department and asked if there was anything they could do to deliver the trees to someone, because late was better than not at all. But the dispatcher told me sorry, no, they were down to a skeleton staff that night.

Disgusted, I finished stuffing the last of my things into my briefcase and headed toward the door.

"Excuse me!" A male voice echoed through the empty office. "Hello! Is anyone here?"

Damn it, I cursed under my breath. I had forgotten to lock the door after the tree guy left.

"Yes, I'm still here."

I turned down the hallway and found a young man standing on the steps.

He was wearing a heavy winter coat, and both his blond hair and the coat were covered in snow.

"I know it's kind of late," he apologized, "but, well, I just suddenly had this funny feeling that maybe you could do something with this."

He stepped aside, and I saw that he had propped a white banana-seat bicycle in the doorway.

I stood there, stunned. Tears welled in my eyes. "You must be an angel," I breathed.

He laughed. "From what she says, my wife sure doesn't think so. But our son outgrew this, and I saw it when I got home from work tonight and went to the basement for the snow shovel. I thought maybe you folks would know of a kid somewhere who could use it."

I began to laugh, and I laughed until tears spilled down my cheeks. "You're not going to believe this," I told him, "but this is the one—the only—gift I was unable to get for one of our foster children. He specifically asked for a white banana-seat bicycle. I'd given up all hope!"

"Well then, here you go! Can I deliver it somewhere for you?"

"No thanks. It'll fit in my car, and I'll stop by the foster parents' on my way home. You just made one little boy very, very happy—and one very tired caseworker too." I held out my hand to him. "I can't thank you enough. Merry Christmas."

"Merry Christmas," he answered, his eyes sparkling.

He loaded the bike into my car, and I delivered it to the surprised foster parents. Later they told me that they had cleaned it up, placed a large red ribbon on it, and had hidden it behind the Christmas tree. When the boy found it the next morning he was overjoyed—but he didn't seem the least bit surprised.

"I knew I was going to get it," he told them when they asked why.

His foster mother asked how he knew.

"An angel told me in a dream. He wore a blue coat and had snow all over him, and he told me not to worry, he would bring me my bike."

I shared the story of the bike's donor with them, and they shook their heads in disbelief.

"Hey," I said smiling. "Don't be so quick to write off angels. After all, I'm looking at two of them right now."

It was without a doubt one of the best Christmas Eves ever.

Of Guns, Bullets, and Farm Sheds

"Hop in!" Bob Morris pushed the police cruiser door open and motioned for me to hurry. The night was dark and cold. I was on call, and my pager had gone off a few minutes ago. When I phoned the dispatcher, she informed me that the deputies were involved in a stand-off with an armed man who had sequestered himself in a house with five children.

"The parents were arrested this evening at a bar for drunk and disorderly conduct; the mother told officers they couldn't arrest her because they had five 'young 'uns' at home."

When deputies went by the house to check on the kids, they were met with gunfire from the children's uncle. The situation was not yet settled, but Bob was hoping to get the kids out and into a foster home quickly. My job, he explained as we sped toward the address, was to act in both my capacity as an EMT and a social worker to make sure the kids were kept safe, unharmed, and calm as they were taken away.

We turned up yet another rutted dirt road into a "holler." The police cruiser careened over deep furrows and rutted potholes. My Toyota would never have made this.

"Enjoying the ride?" Bob grinned in an effort to ease the tension as we blasted through a particularly deep hole.

I had grabbed the door handle to keep from smacking my head on the roof of the car. "Just peachy!" I managed through gritted teeth. "Would you mind going back for my stomach? I think it dropped out about two miles back."

"Unit twenty-three, on location."

We had arrived. A circle of police cruisers and an ambulance filled the trash-strewn yard. Bob pulled on a bulletproof vest, handed me one, then stepped out of the cruiser. "Stay here. I'll call you when we need you. And stay down!" he barked.

"Down?" I asked. "Why?"

The crack of a shotgun, fired from somewhere close by, echoed through the cold night.

"That's why," Bob said grimly.

"Shit!" I cursed as he slammed the door, leaving me alone to cower on the floor of the cruiser. Another shotgun blast sounded, and I closed my eyes, hoping the doors were bulletproof in case a stray shot hit the car.

After what seemed an eternity the car door opened and another officer was crouching beside me. "Mrs. Jacobs? Come on." He grabbed my arm and shepherded me across the moonlit yard. "Keep your head down!" he ordered.

"Where are we going?" I hissed.

"Shh!" He motioned for me to be quiet and follow him. Another shotgun blast sounded from somewhere to my right.

God help me, I thought, beyond terrified, *what have I gotten myself into?*

We scurried, still crouching low, up some rickety wooden steps and onto a large, screened-in porch. Here the officer stopped, still crouching, and motioned for me to head for the door.

"We've got the uncle trapped in a tool shed. The kids are somewhere upstairs."

"Kate?" It was Dilly calling from somewhere inside the house. I slipped through the door and found myself in utter darkness. The all-too-familiar, smoky-sour smell of poverty slammed into me. "Here!" Dilly clicked on a flashlight. "Come on!"

Dilly led the way up a flight of worn wooden stairs. "The kids are upstairs, hiding in the attic. They're fine, just scared. Martin's backing the rig to the door, and as soon as it quiets down outside we'll slip the kids into the ambulance and get them out of here."

"What are they going to do? Shoot the uncle?" I asked, hoping my voice didn't betray the terror I felt.

Dilly stopped and looked out of the window. To my amazement, he began to chuckle. "Doesn't seem that way. Have a look."

I was still crouched down, and now I carefully peeked over the sill of the window on the landing. It took a few moments for my eyes to adjust to the moonlight, but what I saw made some of my terror fade. I could even see a dark sort of humor in the situation.

Down below, one of the deputies was distracting the uncle, who was hunkered in the shed, by talking to him through a bullhorn. In the meantime, two other deputies were scurrying toward the back of the shed with chains and grappling hooks. I watched as the men quietly slid the hooks into the slats of the shed and then motioned to two other officers waiting in their squad cars. There was a roar of engines, and the cars slammed into gear, pulling the chains taut and tearing down the shed wall as they went. The roof teetered for a moment and then fell inward.

I could hear angry screams and curses coming from the pile of wood that had once been the shed.

"You're under arrest!" the officer yelled through the bullhorn.

"Our turn!" said Dilly almost cheerfully.

We scrambled up another flight of stairs and met Bob Morris in the attic. Five redheaded children, including a set of twins, sat huddled together on the floor. The oldest, a girl of perhaps fifteen, eyed me warily.

"What's gonna happen to us?" she asked.

I smiled as reassuringly as I could. "We'll find you a safe place to sleep for the night."

"You're not going to separate us, are you?" she asked with a look of panic.

"I hope not," I answered truthfully. Then it dawned on me. Where on earth was I going to put five children? Every foster home was full!

I mulled this over for a second, and then an idea hit me. "Do you have a telephone?" I asked.

I was relieved when the girl nodded. "In the kitchen."

I asked Dilly if it was safe to turn on the lights, and he radioed down to the deputies.

"Yep. The uncle's in custody," came the crackly response. "Tell Miz Kate to do what she knows best!"

I grinned.

Less than an hour later Sarah showed up at the house. She was armed with cans of soup, a gallon of milk, a dozen donuts, and a loaf of bread. I smiled. Leave it to Sarah, the world's most competent home-help worker, to figure out the family probably didn't have enough food.

After the uncle's arrest, there was no reason to remove the children from the home. While waiting for Sarah, I had put the youngest children back in their beds, then joined Dilly, Martin, and the oldest daughter, Rachel, in the kitchen. Rachel's head was drooping.

"Up you go, my girl," Sarah clucked at her. "It's been far too exciting a night. Off to bed. Mrs. Jacobs here will square away things for you in the morning. I'll stay here and take care of you and the young 'uns tonight."

Rachel nodded, clearly exhausted. "Thank you, ma'am." Sarah put her arm around the girl and led her up to bed.

I climbed into the ambulance with Dilly and Martin, and they dropped me off at my house—an almost forty-minute detour from the station.

"Good night, guys," I said with a yawn.

"You mean good morning," Dilly shot back.

I looked up. Sure enough, the sun was beginning to rise. I was due at work in just a few hours. I sighed. Clearly it was going to be another long, exhausting day.

All Rise for the Honorable Judge John Dawley

I had taken an eleven-year-old boy into custody from school. His arms and legs were covered with welts from a hickory stick, and his eye was black and swollen from a blow delivered by his father. The man had been neither drunk nor under the influence of drugs, and according to the boy, he had "deserved" the beating for sassing his pa. His teacher had tried to explain that no child deserves to be beaten, but the boy still insisted that it was his fault.

When I sat down to interview him at school, he repeated the same sentiments to me. He explained that his father had grown irritated when it took the boy, whose name was Lucas, too long to mow the lawn. Lucas had shot back, "Then why don't you do it yourself!"

Lucas's father had administered the all-too-typical mountain punishment of sending Lucas outside to cut a stout, thumb-thick branch from a nearby hickory tree, then stand still while his father gave him eleven lashings—one for each year of his life. When Lucas tried to squirm out of his father's reach, his father punched him.

"That'll teach you to mind," he said before ordering his son to finish mowing the yard.

The beating was severe enough for me to order Lucas taken into protective custody, and once this was done, I drove him to the hospital to have his face checked. Lucas could not understand why I was not letting him return home, and I made arrangements for him to talk with a local child psychologist.

The next morning I brought the seventy-two-hour protective custody request in front of Judge John Dawley, asking that it be extended until the psychologist could evaluate the family and get the father into anger management therapy.

Judge Dawley was wearing his usual jeans, flannel shirt, and cowboy boots. My colleagues had already warned me that he was being particularly snarky with the social workers that day, and not one of them had gotten him to agree to their case plans.

I sighed and headed into the courtroom where Lucas's father, mother, and the attorney were waiting.

"Afternoon, Hewitt, Mary. Nice to see you," the judge said heartily. "How's that boy of yours?"

I groaned. Clearly Judge Dawley was best pals with the family. In any other court, the judge would rule himself prejudiced and turn the case over to another judge. But not John Dawley.

I shot Patrick a look, and he rolled his eyes. We both knew there was no way we were going to win this hearing. And if we lost, Lucas would lose even worse.

"Mornin', John!" Lucas's father shot back cheerfully. "How's Lynette? Y'all gonna make it to the church social tomorrow night?"

"Wouldn't miss it," the judge answered with a grin. Sobering, he settled himself in his rocking chair, popped a wad of chaw in his mouth, and propped his boots on a stool.

"So what kinda trouble that boy got himself into this time?"

"Your Honor," I said, standing up, "I'd like to present—"

"Quiet, missy!" the judge shot back at me. "I'm not addressin' you. I want to hear from the parents."

"Your Honor, I object!" Patrick stood up.

"Overruled."

The standard protocol for family court hearings was for the caseworkers to present the allegations and what actions had already been taken. Case presentation included police reports, statements from the child or witnesses, photographs, and other evidence to support the reason that the child had been taken into protective custody. The judge then ruled whether the placement had been appropriate, and based on this ruling, the child either remained in protective care or was sent home. We were seeking ongoing placement until the psychological evaluations and a recommendation from the therapist could be made.

I had a photo file of Lucas's injuries and a statement from the emergency room physician that the beating had been severe, as well as his recommendation that the boy remain in protective custody. We were all additionally concerned with Lucas's belief that his beating had been justified.

Now Judge Dawley glared at Patrick. "Your Honor—" Patrick began again.

"I said OVERRULED. Now sit down!" Patrick sat down with a bump.

Lucas's father told his side of the story, and it matched what Lucas had told me.

Judge Dawley listened, nodding all the while. "Waaal," he drawled when Lucas's father finished speaking, "I understand. I go through the same thing with my boy sometimes. The hickory is a fine, simple way to get their attention." He spat his chaw into the spittoon, and I felt my stomach turn over, not only because of his repulsive manners.

"Getting them to cut their own hickory, waaal, it gives 'em time to think about what they did. Good psychology there."

I stifled another groan. I knew exactly where this was going—just as dozens of cases before this one had gone too.

The judge rocked quietly in his chair, hands clasped behind his head, thinking. Presently he fixed his glare on me. "Miz...Jacobs, ain't it?"

I had appeared before him several times a week for the last four years. I knew he knew my name. I bit back my disgust and managed what I hoped was a professional, impassive look.

"Yes, Your Honor."

"Lemme see those pictures."

I approached the bench and handed him the folder. He opened it, thumbed through the contents, closed the folder, and handed it back to me.

"Your Honor, I'd like to ask that these photographs be entered into evidence—"

The judge waved Patrick's comment aside. "Nope."

"Your Honor, this is highly irregular," Patrick protested.

"And I don't want to have to tell you again that this is my court!" the judge shot back.

I could see red creeping up under Patrick's collar, a sure sign that his usual calm temper was beginning to rise. It was my turn to place my hand on Patrick's arm. He sighed, picked up a pencil, and began drumming it on his legal pad.

After a long silence Judge Dawley lowered his legs and sat up. "Tell y'all what," he said, turning to Lucas's parents. "I want you to put that boy in football camp this summer. Coach Bartlett will straighten him right up. Keep usin' a hickory if you need to, but Hewitt, try not to use your fists, all right?"

"Your Honor," I began.

"Your Honor," Patrick chimed in.

"Case dismissed!" Judge Dawley barked.

Lucas's mother shot me a disdainful look as she and her husband got up and shook hands with their attorney. Hewitt went over and shook Judge Dawley's hand, clapped him on the back, and then smiled at me.

"You're just doing your job, honey. I understand."

I gathered up my things and fled the courtroom. One of my co-workers was waiting outside in the hallway to present her case. She caught the look of fury on my face.

"There's nothing you can do about it, Kate," she said gently.

"I know. That's what makes it so awful."

"We've all got to live with him."

"He's a frickin' crook," I spat. "A crooked, disreputable judge!"

She nodded sympathetically. We both knew that Hilary had spoken with the judge often about his behavior and had even gone to the state court to complain, but to no avail.

"I'm afraid we're stuck with him," my co-worker repeated sadly.

"No," I shot back. "We aren't stuck with him—the kids of this county are. And the abuse is never, ever going to stop with the likes of John Dawley on the bench."

I stormed from the courtroom and ran down the outside steps, heading for my office.

Lucas's parents' attorney caught up with me as I was crossing the street.

"No hard feelings?" he asked, grinning at me.

I tried; I tried so hard never to take these cases personally. I did what I could, even though far too often I failed. I had learned incredible patience and temper control with this job, but for some reason, this time I snapped.

I wheeled to face him. "How can you live with yourself?" I shouted. "How can you let Dawley get away with this, knowing this kid is going to get the crap beaten out of him again and again and again?"

"Now, Miz Jacobs—"

"And worse, the kid thinks it's perfectly okay! You're setting him up to be another abusive parent when he grows up!"

He shrugged. "Our legal system is fair. The court hears these cases and makes a ruling. It's a game, sweetheart."

"No," I spat, "it's not a 'game.' It's a sick, demented judge wielding his power over kids who can't defend themselves."

He held up his hands, and I saw that he was still grinning. "Whoa, temper there, little lady!"

"Mr. Paulson, go fuck yourself."

I turned and stormed off. Behind me I heard his roar of laughter.

A Day on the Lake

Dilly and Beth invited Stephan, Virginia, Peter, and me out on their houseboat. It was a hot, humid Sunday in early summer, and we were glad for the chance to escape the heat. Pete and Stephan helped Dilly push off from the dock while Beth, Virginia, and I laid out potato salad, pickles, beer, and sandwich fixings on the table. With a whoop Dilly kicked over the engine, and we set off across the placid lake.

It was beautiful. Dark green pine trees on rolling hills surrounded us, and golden sunshine sparkled off the water. Dilly cruised slowly, stopping periodically to let us dive into the clear blue depths. We spread our towels on the roof of the houseboat and basked in the sun, sipping beer and dozing. Eventually Dilly aimed the boat closer to shore, and we cruised along admiring the beautiful lakefront houses.

"Must be nice to be that rich," Peter mused, gesturing at a rather spectacular home with his beer bottle.

"Hallo! Hallo!" A woman was standing on the dock at the end of a sloping lawn belonging to an equally impressive house nearby, waving frantically in our direction. "Help! Oh please, help!"

"What the...?" Dilly quickly revved the engine and turned the boat toward the dock.

When we pulled closer we could see a teenage boy lying on the dock writhing in pain. When Dilly cut the engine we could hear his groans. While Peter and Stephan secured the boat, Dilly and I leaped onto the dock.

"My son," the woman gasped, "he's hurt! He stepped out with one foot on the sailboat, but it moved away from the dock and he did…he did a split…"

Dilly and I examined the boy quickly. It was a classic case of hip dislocation caused by a sudden, violent "split" of both legs. His had been pulled apart as the boat and the dock separated. The boy's right leg was markedly shorter than the left, his right knee was bent at an unnatural angle, and the leg and foot were rotated inward—a classic indicator of a probable femoral head fracture. This was a very serious and horribly painful injury and ran the risk of necrosis, or "death," of the femur head without immediate surgical intervention. The result could be permanent crippling of the leg. This was one injury where time was of the essence.

"I'll radio for an ambulance, ma'am," Dilly told the woman, heading for the boat's wheelhouse.

I called up to Pete to bring me an icepack and a blanket so I could secure the boy's hip. The poor kid was groaning in agony. He gripped my hand.

"I'm Kate," I told him gently. "Dilly and I are with the Highton Fire Department."

"Th-thanks," he gasped. "I'm J-John."

At that moment the boy's father came storming out of the sprawling house and onto the deck. He was chomping on an unlit cigar and glared at us when he arrived. "What the hell is going on here?" he demanded.

My jaw dropped. It was Judge John Dawley.

After my initial shock, a surprising calm washed over me, and I stood up to face the judge. He wasn't a judge here; he was just another person, and his son was badly hurt.

"Your son broke his hip," I explained. "The boat's captain and I are both EMTs with the Highton Fire Department. Dilly is radioing for an ambulance."

Judge Dawley eyed me coldly. I got the feeling he didn't recognize me. Four years of standing in his courtroom and he had no idea who I was.

"We don't need an ambulance," he snapped. "I'll drive the boy myself."

"No, sir," I said firmly. "Your son probably has a femoral head fracture.

He needs to go on a backboard in exactly the position he's in and get to the hospital as fast as possible."

Judge Dawley pulled the cigar from his mouth, leaned over his son, eyed him disdainfully, and then lightly kicked the boy's injured hip with his boot. The boy screamed.

"You sound like a girl! Shut up and get up, you sissy!" Judge Dawley bellowed.

Dilly was not a small man, and he towered a full head over Judge Dawley. While the rest of us looked on in horror he leaped out of the houseboat and crossed the dock in two strides to grab the judge by the collar of his shirt.

"Back off!" he shouted, red-faced. "Back off now! And don't you ever, ever let me catch you treating your boy like that again!"

Dawley stared levelly into Dilly's eyes. "Let me go, son. Let me go and we'll pretend this never happened. That is, unless you want to be charged with assault."

"And I'll see you're charged with child abuse."

Dawley laughed out loud. "In this county? That'll be the day!"

With a sinking feeling, I knew he was right. "Dilly—" I warned.

Instantly Dilly let go of the judge. But he wasn't about to ignore his duties as an EMT. "Back off," he said again through clenched teeth. "Your boy is going on a backboard, and that's final."

The judge was at least smart enough not to argue further with Dilly about that. And I felt it would be best if I took myself out of the picture. Pete brought the blanket, pillow, and an icepack while I quietly slipped back onto the boat.

It didn't take too long for an ambulance to arrive, and Dilly helped secure John and load him up. His mother got in the ambulance with her son; his father did not.

We didn't speak until the boat was well out on the lake. Dilly shook his head in disbelief. "He's the family court judge? Jesus!"

"It explains a lot," I said quietly. "It explains a whole lot."

If Judge John Dawley had recognized me out there on the dock he had given no sign, and I had thought it best to keep my mouth shut. At least I now fully understood what we faced in family court: a man who was a child abuser himself ruling over the fate of all the abused kids in the county.

God help them all.

Fire and Brimstone?

I was sanctimonious enough to believe that I was above prejudice. After all, I had waged my own private anti-racism war in Paul Braxton's clinic by eliminating the segregated waiting rooms, treating all patients with respect by calling them *Mr.* or *Mrs.*, and always verbally blasting anyone who dared use the "N-word" around me.

But really, how diverse was my circle of friends? Every one of us was cauliflower white. And how comfortable would I be if I suddenly found myself in a social gathering where I was in the minority and not the other way around?

I readily admit that I had looked down on the patients I'd helped treat years ago who had been crippled by the supposed curse of voodoo spells. After all, how could anyone be so ignorant as to fall for such nonsense?

My racist demons reared their ugly heads on a warm, sunny summer afternoon when I found myself confronted by one of our foster mothers during a picnic. Her name was Nona Davies. She was as round as she was tall and had a heart to match. But she was strict, incredibly strict, and she was well known in our office as a force to be reckoned with.

One "look" from Nona could compel even the most difficult foster child into instant obedience. Nona set her own rules as to how her home was run, and not only the children placed with her but every single social worker had better abide by them—or else!

I had no idea what the *or else* might be, but I knew one thing for sure: I did not want to find out.

Even Judge Dawley treated Nona with a form of grudging respect and went along with the recommendations she made for the care and treatment of her foster children or their parents. That's because Nona often snapped, "that's horse piles!" to an order Judge Dawley handed down.

Eventually, rather than go into one of his "this is my court" tirades, he would eye Nona warily and say, "Waal then, Miz Nona. What do you recommend?"

She then spoke her mind, and to everyone's astonishment, the judge simply nodded and said, "So be it."

"Holy shit," my co-worker Laura had whispered to me the first time we witnessed this. "I wish I had that power over the beast!"

"The beast" was probably the least unkind moniker we used for Judge John Dawley.

It's true that Nona ruled her home, and our caseloads, with an iron fist. And it was true that no one dared say no to Nona.

On that pretty summer day we were having a picnic for all of our foster kids. There were balloons, games, a slip-n-slide, even pony rides arranged by a neighbor of mine. We dished up donated hotdogs, hamburgers, ice cream, and cake, and my co-workers and I had brought along guitars, dulcimers, and banjos to lead the kids in a series of folksongs.

During the sing-along, the smallest ones sat in the grass at our feet, and one three-year-old climbed into my lap despite my guitar and listened in rapt attention as I played a solo.

The song was one of my favorites: "What Color is God's Skin?"

> Goodnight, I said to my little one so tired out when the day was done.
> Then she said as I tucked her in, "Tell me, Daddy, what color is God's skin?"
> I said, "It is black, it is yellow, it is red, and it is white—every child is the same in the good Lord's sight."[1]

Nona was sitting in a lawn chair, her hips spilling over the sides, watching. When the song was done, she pointed at me. "You're comin' to my church on Sunday and singin' that song!" It was not a request; it was an order.

Me? Attend an AME church? Me, a lone white woman, attend a service with an all-black congregation? I felt my fear demons rise. "I, um, Miss Nona, well, thank you," I mumbled, "but I don't sing well enough to—"

Nona cut me off. "Ten o'clock sharp. In fact, you get there ten minutes early!"

"I, um, yes, ma'am," I mumbled.

Several of the older kids giggled. Nona shot them one of her "looks," and they fell silent, but I could read the laughter in their eyes. Little beasts. They were no doubt delighting in the fact that Miss Nona scared adults as much as she did the kids.

***

On Sunday morning Pete sat in bed watching as I tried on outfit after outfit. The bedroom was a mess, with clothes, stockings, and shoes strewn everywhere.

"Oh, come on, Kate!" he grumbled as yet another frock landed on the floor. "You're going to a church, not a meeting with the president of the United States!"

"What am I supposed to wear? These people dress like peacocks when they attend church," I fumed. (Racial discrimination, anyone?) Pete snorted and turned over to go back to sleep. He was not coming with me, and he had made it clear that he was not happy with me giving up another Sunday to deal with CPS clients, even for Sunday worship. Our marriage was rocky, and things like this weren't helping.

I finally settled on a periwinkle-blue sundress with a cream bolero jacket and sling-back sandals. I hoped it wasn't too loud.

I needn't have worried. When I arrived at the church a whole fifteen minutes early, Nona was already waiting for me outside the modest whitewashed building. Her huge frame had been stuffed into a brilliant scarlet frock. She wore a red feathered hat on her head, bright red shoes, white gloves, and carried a matching red sequined handbag.

She eyed me as I approached and then nodded. "A bit conservative, Miss Kate, but it'll do."

I suspected that, coming from Nona, this was high praise indeed.

"Where's your guitar, Kate Jacobs?" Nona demanded next.

"Well, er, I forgot it."

Actually no, I hadn't. I had conveniently left it at home as a way to wriggle out of having to sing in church. My voice really, really was not that good. Singing to a handful of young foster kids was one thing; singing in front of an entire church congregation was another.

"No matter," Nona said firmly. "There are plenty here."

My heart sank to my knees. Nona simply grunted, wrapped her huge arm around me, and propelled me into the church.

I had been raised a Lutheran, and throughout my childhood, my parents had pounded "church manners" into my siblings and me. Going to church in the fifties and sixties meant dressing up: a dark suit and tie for my father and brothers, conservative dresses or a skirt and blouse with low-heeled pumps and white gloves for my mother, my sister, and me.

It meant sitting quietly on a hard wooden bench without fidgeting while listening to a seemingly endless sermon, doing a lot of praying, singing a mournful hymn or two, and shaking hands and making polite conversation with the other parishioners outside the church door after the service. Church, I had long ago decided, was formal, standoffish, and thoroughly dull.

No doubt that was why I was utterly unprepared for Miss Nona's.

"Hallelujah!" Reverend Avery Jessup began at the top of his lungs as he strode to the podium in his flowing purple robes. "Hallelujah and praise the Lord God Almighty for this beautiful day! This is a day the Lord has made, rejoice with me in it!"

"Praise the Lord!"

"Bless you, Jesus!"

"Amen! Amen!"

The shouts of affirmation around me were deafening. Because Nona sang in the church choir, she had abandoned me at the beginning of the service to the care of one of her church "sisters," a reed-thin woman in shimmering white satin with the darkest skin I had ever seen. A pillbox hat with white netting was perched on her head, and she had studied my own bare head with a frown when we were introduced

"Hmm," she'd said, then fished a beautifully embroidered lace handkerchief out of her handbag. She placed this on top of my head and secured it with a bobby pin. "There, that's better."

"I'm sorry," I had stammered, "I didn't realize I needed to cover my head."

"Why, no, child, you don't. But how on earth you gonna get God's attention if you dress so demure?"

She had laughed as she took my arm and steered me through a throng of shimmering satin-clad worshippers to a pew near the front. "This is a house of joy!"

Even in my bright blue dress I felt dull and conservative compared to the churchgoers around me. In fact, I had never seen such an array of colorful clothes. Forget the dark, conservative attire of my fellow Lutherans. Even the men here were brightly clothed, wearing suits in shining peacock blue, cherry red, emerald green, and gold. The women wore satin and sported hats with riotous feathers, jewels, and netting. I'd never seen anything so ostentatious— or so beautiful.

After Reverend Jessup's greeting, the choir launched into a boisterous spiritual hymn. Everyone around me erupted into song and leaped to their feet. They clapped and rocked and shouted "Hallelujah!" and "Amen!" throughout the singing. The choir was good, really good. I felt myself pulled up by the rhythm, and I got to my feet and clapped along.

"Ah can't hear you!" the minister, who also served as the choir director, shouted.

"Amen!" The responding shout was deafening.

"What?!" he roared back.

"Amen!"

"And again!"

"Amen!"

Perhaps the best word to define Nona's congregation was joyous. Joy flowed through us, swirled around us, soared to the rafters and back to the pews. It overflowed the aisles and altar. The shouts of "amen," the singing, the dancing, and the clapping were all joyous affirmations of faith, of belief, of love. The bright clothing and garish hats were a rainbow of celebration, a reflection of joyous lives lived in God's name. I compared this to my childhood church and realized how alive this church felt.

When the song ended, everyone sat down, and Reverend Jessup approached the podium. "We have a visitor with us today. I want you all to rise and give a warm welcome to Miz Kate Jacobs!"

The minister's voice cut into my musings, and my face grew hot as the entire congregation rose and began belting out a song of welcome. When they quieted down, the minister turned his attention fully on me. I wanted to squirm under the pew.

"Welcome, Miz Kate."

"Th-thank you," I managed.

"I understand this is your first time in our church. Is that right?"

"Yes, sir," I mumbled.

"What? Child, I can't hear you!"

"Yes, SIR!" I said louder.

Several people laughed.

Reverend Jessup grinned. "And to what church do you belong?"

"Um, I'm Lutheran, sir."

"Lutheran, eh? Don't worry, we'll pray for you, won't we!" He was grinning, teasing me.

"I would appreciate that, sir. I need all the praying for I can get."

The minister burst out laughing. Then he said a prayer—a prayer I will never forget and one that I would think about all too often in the not-so-distant future when it felt as if my entire world was disintegrating around me.

He knew a surprising amount about the work I did and about the children in foster care. He prayed for my co-workers and me; for our strength to endure the trials of the work God had no doubt commanded us to do. He prayed for strength for the hardships he knew were to come (boy, did he get that right!) and, astonishingly, for God to open the blind eyes and hearts of those who could not find it in them to help the lost children of Highton County.

How on earth did he know?

"And God," he prayed, "there are those powers of darkness that be watchin' this woman; watchin' and tryin' to stand in her way—in your way.

Guard her now and keep her safe as you did before. Shine your silver light over her; pull her into your sphere of light, protection, and safety...just as you've done before."

I felt a chill. Was it possible—? But how could he have known?

I'd never told anyone, not even Pete, about what had happened in the car wreck, about the silver bubble that had seemed to surround me. Virginia was the only other person on earth who knew what had happened because she'd been there, and ever since the day we'd briefly mentioned its existence, we had forged an unspoken agreement never to talk about it again.

But now this AME minister was referring to what could only be the experience we'd both been through when my ancient Volkswagen slammed into that school bus. But was he really? Surely he was speaking euphemistically?

Then Nona was calling me up to sing. To my great relief, she didn't embarrass me by asking me to sing alone. In fact, the choir knew the song, and the congregation rose as one to sing "What Color is God's Skin?"

The service ended with "Amazing Grace." Afterward, the parishioners filed out for lunch in the commons hall.

Reverend Jessup shook my hand warmly as I left. Bending down unexpectedly, he kissed my cheek and whispered for only me to hear: "You be careful, child. There's darkness following you. We'll be keepin' you in our prayers."

Surprised and somewhat embarrassed, I managed only a smile and a weak thank you. Maybe he thought Satan himself was nipping at my heels?

It wasn't until much later that I came to understand the gravity of his warning.

The CAFC

The group called itself the CAFC: The Crimes Against Families Coalition. They were a collection of child abusers who had run afoul of the family court system. Most had had their parental rights terminated, others were currently enmeshed in the Child Protective Services system; all of them believed that it was within their "God-given rights" to raise their children in the way they saw fit. "Spare the rod and spoil the child" was their typical motto. Some even believed that it was within a father's rights to introduce his daughters to sexuality.

We called them the "Crazies and Fruit Cakes Coalition." They had their own attorneys who routinely represented them in court because they didn't trust public defenders or, for that matter, any "secular" attorney.

The CAFC attorneys began each hearing by falling to their knees and praying that God would intervene and allow his righteous sheep to win against the heathen, barbarian secularists. Even Judge Dawley was disgusted by them, but he allowed their shenanigans to go on in the courtroom. I personally believed that Dawley was, for all his bluff and bluster, a coward.

Hilary had called me into her office that particular morning to hand me a thin folder. "I'd like you to take a look at this new intake, Kate," she said matter-of-factly.

In the folder was an intake form listing the names of four children, aged six to fourteen. There was no other information, no allegation, no name of the person who had made the report, no address, nothing.

I looked at Hilary, perplexed. "I'm not sure what you want me to do with this," I said.

Hilary leaned back in her chair. "This is a highly unusual case. I'll tell you only that it's been through the wringer. Countless caseworkers have interviewed these children, and the case has been in and out of our legal system for a very long time." She sighed and wearily rubbed her temples. "It came to us from a neighboring county. In fact, it's crossed several state lines. Kate, you are the best child sexual assault interviewer we have. I need you to interview these kids."

"Based on what?" I asked.

"I know this is going to sound very odd, but based on nothing. I want you to know nothing about these kids or what they may or may not have gone through or what's being alleged. I just want you to go in completely blind and see what you think."

I had never heard of such a thing, but I confess Hilary's off-handed compliment had puffed up my ego, so I agreed. Hilary smiled at me. The woman knew her stuff and how to get her staff to take on even the worst challenges.

I met with the Townsend children the next morning. A guardian ad litem had brought them in, which in itself was unusual. GALs are court-appointed advocates who stand in support of the children. They don't care about the needs or wishes of a child's parents, the courts, or the social workers. They represent the child's best interests alone. They do their own investigating, interviewing, and research; they make their own recommendations to the court. Usually those recommendations equate with ours, and only rarely do the CPS and the GALs clash. However, when they do, they usually clash with the parents.

This particular GAL smiled at me and without a word nodded for the youngest child, the six-year-old girl, to go with me. She did so, and we sat down at the table in the interview room. This too was a little unusual since I always used a combination playroom/interview room when I talked with kids. Children invariably headed for the toys while adults or teens headed for the sofa or the table and chairs.

"Annie," I said after introducing myself, "do you know why you're here?"

She nodded and said very matter-of-factly and in a very grown-up voice, "Yes. Because my mom says our dad sex-shual-ly..." she pronounced the word deliberately and carefully, "abused us." She stopped and looked up at me. I waited for her to go on.

When she remained silent, I said, "And is that true?"

"Nope."

"Sweetheart, do you know what 'sexually abused' means?"

Annie began kicking the table leg rhythmically. "Yup. It means you get touched on the private parts, or somebody makes you touch them on their private parts."

"That's a pretty good definition," I said. "Why would your mommy think that happened to you?"

"Mommy hates Daddy," she said simply. "Daddy loves us and wants us to live with him, not with her."

I was beginning to see the light. This was a custody dispute—an ugly one. Still, I kept that thought to myself and warned myself not to jump to conclusions.

"Annie, my job is to take care of kids and be sure that nobody hurts them. If somebody is abusing you in any way, I can make it stop. Lots of kids tell me about being touched. Lots of kids tell other grownups they love and trust if they're being hurt or touched in any way they don't like. If somebody touched you or made you uncomfortable, who could you tell?"

"Daddy."

"Could you tell Mommy too?"

Annie stopped kicking the table and fixed her cool gaze on me. "Nope."

"No? Why not?"

"Because Mom is curraazzeeee."

"Can you tell me a bit more about that?" I prodded gently.

"Mommy hit us. Daddy got mad and took us away."

"Mommy hit you..."

Bang, bang, bang. Her foot started making contact with the table leg again. "A big blue broom—whack, smack, whack, carrrack!"

I waited for her to go on.

"Danny called Daddy. Daddy came and got us." She looked up at me. "How come everybody keeps askin' us? I don't want to talk about it anymore."

"You don't have to tell me if you don't want to."

"Okay." Annie got up and headed for the door.

Danny came in next. He was almost eleven, and he shook my hand solemnly before he sat down.

"Hi, Danny. I'm—"

He cut me off. "Yeah, I know. Another social worker."

"Sounds like you've seen a lot of us lately."

He sighed heavily. "You got no idea."

"No," I agreed. "I don't. Usually when I go somewhere to talk to kids, or they come in and talk to me, I know a little bit about them. Honestly, I know absolutely nothing about you guys except your names and how old you are."

"Humph." Danny went over and picked up a Nerf ball, which he began to toss against the two-way mirror.

"So how many people are watching this time?"

"You mean behind the mirror glass?"

"Uh-huh."

"Nobody. Go check if you want. You get into the mirror room through that door." I pointed.

He got up and peered into the tiny room behind the mirror that the detectives often used when I was interviewing sexual assault victims. Today it was empty.

Danny shut the door, shrugged, and picked up the ball again.

"I'm sorry you have to be here, Danny."

"If you want to know if our dad abused us, the answer is no. No, no, no. Dad is great. Mom is nuts, totally bonkers nuts."

"What makes her nuts?" I asked.

He stopped throwing the ball and looked at me. "She drinks. She goes to this church and they make her pray all the time. Mom says we have the devil in us. She says she has to hit the devil out."

I looked at him quizzically and motioned for him to toss the ball to me. He lobbed it, I missed it.

Danny laughed. "You suck."

"Yep. I can't throw, and I can't catch."

"So what can you do?"

"Take care of kids. Help them when they're in trouble."

"Can you get us back with our dad?"

"Well, I guess that depends on you. I can't help you if I don't know what's going on."

"We're in a foster home, you know."

"No, I didn't know."

Danny mulled that over for a while. Then he sat down and looked at me solemnly. "I'm going to tell you what I told the other social workers. Nobody touched us like that."

"Meaning?"

"Private parts. Nobody. Not Dad, nobody. Dad would never do that, never. He left Mom 'cause of her drinking and her stupid church. And she hit us. A lot. With a spoon, a stick, a rug beater, then a broom. That's when Dad finally came and got us. Mom wants us back. She told us to tell that Dad was touching us. But it ain't true."

"I believe you."

"You do?"

"Yup. It's my job to believe kids."

"Weird!"

"No, it really isn't. I find kids to be much more honest than adults."

"So if I said again my mom beat us, you'd believe it?"

I smiled. "Try me."

"Well, she did. She had this blue broom. She beat the crap out of Annie and Dave with it and broke Dave's head open."

I winced.

"Dave grabbed the broom when she was hitting Annie, so she started to beat him with it. He laughed at her. That got her even madder, so she hit harder. Busted his head open and his nose too."

"Where was Annie during all this?"

"Hiding under the kitchen table."

Danny stopped talking and looked at me. "Can we go home now, please? Please?"

"Where is home?"

"With Dad."

I smiled at him reassuringly. "Just one more question, if you don't mind." I held a huge box of crayons out to him. "Do me a favor—pick the crayon that most closely matches the color of the broom."

Danny looked at me as if I was crazy, shrugged, and chose a robin's egg blue crayon and handed it to me.

"Thanks," I said. I put it back in the box.

"Are you going to let us go home?"

"I'll do my best, Danny. I promise."

The oldest son, David, came in next. He flopped down in one of the overstuffed armchairs and sighed. "Here we go again."

"Hi, Dave. I'm Kate."

"Interviewer number seven hundred and fifty."

"That many, huh?"

"Feels like it." He scowled at me.

"So why don't you tell me what's going on, because honestly, other than what Danny and Annie told me, I'm totally in the dark."

"Well, it's simple. Mom and Dad split because of Mom's drinking and hitting us. Then Mom totally lost it and beat the crap out of Annie. I tried to stop her, but she whaled me too. Danny called Dad. He came and got us. Then Mom accused Dad of sexually molesting us."

"Did he?" I asked.

"Hell, no! Mom lied!"

"I believe you."

David eyed me in surprise.

"Dave," I asked, learning forward, "I know you've told this story a hundred times. Can you just kind of fill me in on exactly what happened the day your dad took you?"

David repeated the same story Annie and Danny had told me. He threw in quite a few more details—how the brawl had sent the cat flying across the kitchen table, knocking a bottle of milk, the sugar, and several plates to the floor. That had made his mother even madder.

"How badly were you hurt when she hit you?" I asked.

"Busted my nose, split my head." He leaned forward and parted his hair, showing me a two-inch scar in his scalp.

"I'm sorry that happened to you," I said softly.

Dave shrugged. "I'd rather get smacked by Ma again than have to live without Dad."

His jaw clenched, and the bravado faded. The tough-young-teen look disappeared, and I saw a frightened and defeated child glaring at me through clear blue eyes. I leaned forward and rested my hand on his shoulder.

"I can't even imagine how hard this has been on you, and I'm sorry to have to ask you to talk about it again." I waited, allowing David time to collect his thoughts. "What happened next?"

He sighed. "Dad got us. He reported Mom to CPS. They placed us with Dad and told Mom she could only have supervised visits with us. The next thing we know Mom accused Dad of molesting us. It's bullshit, total bullshit."

"If you could wave a magic wand and make things perfect, how would your life look?"

David leaned forward. "For us to be home with Dad and for Mom and her fruitcake church friends to go away forever."

I nodded. "David, one more thing." I handed him the box of crayons. "Can you show me what color the broom was that she hit you with? Which crayon matches it most?"

Out of the dozens of crayons in the box, he chose the same robin's egg blue as his brother.

"Why's that important?" he asked me.

"Details," I smiled. "Details."

The fourth child, nine-year-old Hank, refused to be interviewed. I respected his wishes. The only thing he would say to me was, "Dad never touched us."

I gave my report to Hilary that same evening. "Well?" she asked when I tapped on her office door.

"The Townsend kids?" I reminded her.

"Ah yes," she said, motioning for me to sit down.

I handed her the report I had written up, but she didn't open it. "What are your thoughts, Kate?"

"Dad isn't abusing them. Mom is, or has."

Hilary smiled slightly. "That's what three other social workers ahead of you found too."

I wasn't surprised. "Did the kids undergo a forensic physical?"

"Yes."

"And?"

"They found that the two youngest had reddened rectums and Annie had a bit of unspecific vaginitis. So the suspicion is obviously there."

"Hmm. Is there any chance I can interview the dad?"

"Sure." Hilary pulled another sheet of paper out of a file on her desk. "He lives in South Carolina, near Spartanburg. He fled with the kids to his parents' home in Minnesota for a while, but the court ordered him back. He's been very compliant."

"Did he undergo a sexual deviancy eval?"

"Yep. Plethysmograph, polygraph. Passed them both. He's clean."

A penile plethysmograph is a device that measures changes in blood flow to the penis and is used to assess sexual arousal and orientation. Though the results aren't admissible in court, they can reveal a lot, such as whether an alleged perpetrator is sexually aroused by children.

"And the case is still open why?"

"The CAFC is threatening a lawsuit if we don't give the kids back to the mother. They also insist that prior social workers were prejudiced."

I snorted.

The next day I made the long drive to South Carolina to visit Lawrence Townsend, the kids' dad. He was a big, blond man, and I could see David's and Danny's faces clearly in his. He had been expecting me, and we sat down on his porch.

Lawrence repeated pretty much what the kids had told me—that he had left home because he could no longer take his wife's drinking and the fact that she was beating the kids with a wooden spoon. A few nights after he left, Danny called him. The boy was hysterical and told him that their mother had just beaten David and Annie with a broom and had broken David's nose.

"I had no idea she would ever go that far. I went right away and got them. A few days later a report was filed against me, alleging I was sexually abusing the kids." He rubbed his hands over his face. "I can't imagine why anyone would think..." His voice trailed off. There were tears in his eyes.

On the long drive south to his home I'd endlessly reviewed the few things I'd learned about the case. "Mr. Townsend," I suddenly asked, "do the kids take showers or baths when they're here with you?"

"David showers, the others bathe," he answered. "Why?"

"Mind if I see your bathroom?"

He shrugged and led me down the hall to a tiny, old-fashioned bathroom with a claw-footed tub. I looked around. On the shelf above the tub was a box of Mr. Sudzy bubble bath powder.

"The kids use this stuff?"

"Annie does."

"You might think about getting rid of it," I told him slowly and deliberately. "It's an irritant and can cause unspecific vaginitis in girls. It irritates mucus membranes," I explained.

Lawrence Townsend didn't respond for a moment, but then all at once he began to grin. "Thanks," he said. "Thanks so much!"

The following week I was called in to testify at the Townsend children's hearing. Patrick and I took our usual seats at the prosecutor's table. Lawrence Townsend and his attorney sat at a table beside us, and a pretty, plump woman with bright red hair sat at a table to their left. Beside her were two women I had never seen before. Both wore loose-fitting gray suits and clunky, lace-up orthopedic shoes; both had very long gray hair and both, I swore, had identical faces that reminded me of the evil witch from *The Wizard of Oz*.

I leaned over to Patrick and whispered, "Who the hell are they?"

"The CAFC attorneys," he explained.

"Good God! Why on earth are they dressed like Halloween witches?"

Patrick grinned. "Because they are."

The case was being heard by Judge Gerald Fox, and we rose as he entered the courtroom. The bailiff called the court in session. Then, to my horror, the two CAFC attorneys rose, stepped before the bench, and fell to their knees. One began to pray loudly, begging God to oversee these proceedings and help the judge rule in a way that was good and right and to protect their poor sister from the abuses she had been subject to.

What about the kids? I wondered as the shock wore off. *Why aren't you praying for them?*

Judge Fox waited for another moment then banged loudly with his gavel. "This court is in session," he said firmly. "In the future, please do your praying beforehand."

"Your Honor, we—" one of the witches began.

"You have not been called to the bench! Sit down or I'll have you removed from my court."

My lips twitched. I couldn't help it. *Don't laugh*, I ordered myself, *whatever you do, don't laugh.*

The hearing took up most of the morning. The children's mother testified that she had always suspected her husband was sexually molesting them but had been too afraid to turn him in. She emphatically denied hitting the children.

The sexual deviancy specialist testified that he had seen no evidence of pedophilia in Lawrence Townsend. He added that the father's polygraph results upheld the father's denial of the allegations.

We broke for lunch and reconvened later that day. It was my turn to testify. Judge Fox had the bailiff swear me in, and the questioning began. I repeated my findings of the interview and my conclusion.

One of the witches rose and stood in front of me. "Mrs. Johnson—"

I ignored the error. I knew full well it was just a distractive ploy.

"Just how many children have you interviewed regarding sexual abuse issues?"

I sat for a moment and made a few mental calculations. By now I had been in the field for more years than I liked to consider.

"Several thousand."

The attorney looked taken aback.

"You interviewed the Townsend children last week. You only interviewed them once, is that correct?"

"That is correct."

"And you received a full report on these children prior to the interview disclosing supposed earlier findings beforehand, didn't you?"

"No, I did not. I was asked to interview these children blind, with no prior history, no allegations, and knowing only their names and ages."

She looked startled, and it dawned on me that this woman was completely unprepared.

"Your report states that you found no evidence that these children were sexually abused but that they were physically abused by their mother."

"That's a LIE!" the children's mother screeched, springing to her feet.

"Order!" Judge Fox said firmly. "Order or I'll have you removed from this court!"

Mrs. Townsend sat down, glaring at the judge.

The witch continued, "You determined this after one interview. How do you know the children weren't lying? I have statements from members of the church that the children are habitual liars."

"Objection, Your Honor! Hearsay!" Patrick said loudly.

"Sustained. Mrs. Jacobs, please continue."

"I can't speak to that, ma'am, but I can speak to what I found."

"After one interview—one interview and no other contact—you *determined*," she bit the last word off sarcastically, "that these children had been beaten by their mother."

"Yes, ma'am."

"Oh, this should be good," she sneered. "Pray do tell us how you came to this conclusion in only one interview."

"I interviewed the children separately, using standard non-leading interview techniques. Basically that means I don't ask leading questions, I just let the children tell me in their own words what happened. Their stories matched."

"And how do you know they didn't collaborate on their stories and rehearse them beforehand? They had plenty of time to do so."

"Details," I said calmly, thinking about that blue crayon. "Each child was able to fill in a great deal of detail. In collaborated or rehearsed stories, children can't deviate far from their script. Each of these children told me what happened from their perspective. While not exactly identical, their stories matched. I also asked them questions about details to try and trip them up. They were solid."

The witch snorted. "And what would you say if I told you that there was physical evidence that the children had been sexually abused?"

"I would need to know what that evidence is, ma'am."

"Upon examination by both a physician and the mother, the youngest boy was found to have a reddened rectum, the girl vaginitis," she spat.

"Unspecified vaginitis, according to the report."

The CAFC attorney looked triumphant. "Oh! So you *have* read it!"

"After I interviewed the children," I explained.

"And what do you know about vaginitis and abuse?" the woman sneered at me.

I leaned slightly forward in the witness chair. "The medical report, if you'll read it, states that her hymen was intact and there was no evidence of penetration. Additionally, there was unspecified vaginitis—basically vulvar irritation. This can be caused by soap or by rubbing on, say, a bicycle seat, improper wiping when using the toilet, or in the case of Annie Townsend, the use of Mr. Sudzy bubble bath, which I know she was using. In the boy Danny's case, the reddened rectum could easily be indicative of straining over a hard stool, bubble bath irritation, diarrhea—lots of things. There were no indicators of rectal penetration in the report."

"Is that right?" the CAFC witch spat. "But you aren't medically trained to make such a determination, are you?"

I shot Patrick a look and saw that he was trying his darndest not to grin.

"Oh, but I am. I'm a registered nurse and have been a practicing emergency medical technician for the past decade. I've been trained in and worked in family practice, including obstetrics and gynecology, emergency medicine, and I've assisted in several hundred forensic child sexual assault examina—"

"That will be ENOUGH!" the CAFC attorney shrieked. "No further questions!"

Patrick's grin was now so wide it appeared to take up his whole face. "Know your witness," he mouthed at me. I grinned back.

It didn't take Judge Fox long to reach his conclusion. He ordered the children to be returned to their father's custody and for the mother to undergo a full psychiatric evaluation. He revoked her visitation rights until such a time as a court-appointed psychiatrist deemed it safe for supervised visits to occur. The case against the father was closed.

"This is a CRIME!" the CAFC attorney who had interviewed me shouted when the judge's gavel banged for the last time. She fell to her knees and began praying loudly: "Oh Lord, forgive these heathens! They know not what they do! Strike your righteousness into their black hearts—"

"Out!" Judge Fox barked. "Get out of my courtroom! Bailiff!"

The bailiff stepped forward and dragged the still praying women away.

"You have not heard the end of this!" one of them shouted from the door. "You have NOT!"

I'd like to be able to say that because of me and my excellent interviewing skills, sleuthing, and any other swell-headed form of self-aggrandizement, the CAFC lost the case, but the truth was that the case had already been decided long before. I was simply a symbolic pawn, a sop, as it were, appointed by the courts at the demand of the CAFC. (Incidentally, I would have other hearings with the witches in the future, and they would begin to voir dire me regularly. I took it as a compliment.)

With the hearing over, I packed my briefs then headed out to find the Townsends. The kids were waiting with their father and the GAL in the prosecutor's office. I stepped in and shut the door. The children jumped to their feet, Annie clinging to her father's hand. They looked at me fearfully.

"Go home," I smiled. "Go home with your dad."

There was a whoop and a shout, and four bodies hurled themselves at me. There were tears in Lawrence Townsend's eyes. He took my hands in his big paws. "God bless you, Kate Jacobs," he said softly. "God bless you."

"It wasn't me," I said simply. "It was your four brave, honest kids and a lot of other social workers who did most of the legwork before me."

A month later I received a framed photo of the Townsend kids and their dad in the mail. I smiled as I set it on my desk. Maryann Tevis was right. Sometimes things did work out for the best.

Of Beelzebub and Bunnies

I stared at the intake form in my hand and tried once again to make sense of the directions. *Park at the top of the holler road. Go in through the pasture (gate on the right-hand side of the watering trough—be sure to close gate behind you). Cross the pasture, but keep along the fence line to avoid Beelzebub. The cabin is the second one down the forest path to your right.*

There were two footpaths leading to two fences on my right, as well as two gates and two watering troughs. Did the directions mean the pasture on the right or the one on the left with the gate on the right? Both paths cut across pastureland and ended at a dense stand of hickory and oak. Which one was I supposed to take?

I looked around, weighing my options and squinting in the bright sunshine that shimmered across the humid fields. In one of the pastures a herd of cows had stopped grazing and were staring at me, heads lifted. The other pasture was empty. I looked at the directions again, clueless.

The intake had been coded as "immediate"; the postpartal (after birth) nurse at Highton County General had reported that the mother of a premature baby had left the hospital against medical advice and taken her son home to the holler "where Will'n me'll do just fine carin' fer him." The mother had refused home-health intervention.

Concerned about the fragile infant, the hospital had requested Child Protective Services to check on him. Given my nursing background, Hilary had asked if I would take the case and give the premature baby a "once over."

Now I stared again at the directions in my hand, wondering what "avoiding Beelzebub" meant. Finally I chose the empty pasture on the far right. I hoisted my briefcase across one shoulder and the bag of supplies, including a portable neonatal scale, tins of baby formula, bottles, a measuring tape, and postpartal vitamins, across the other. Recent heavy rains had left the path muddy, and the gate stuck as I attempted to push it open.

Stupidly I was wearing a long skirt and sandals. I had learned in the early weeks of this job to always keep a set of hiking boots and jeans in my car, but I had worn them to a home visit the day before, gotten them muddy, and forgot to put them back in the car after cleaning them.

I finally gave up, climbed over the gate, and picked my way across the soggy field toward the footpath that led into the trees. Dragonflies flitted around me, and the hot air echoed with the scratchy song of cicadas. I swatted at a buzzing horsefly that seemed determined to take a chunk out of my skin, tore the hem of my skirt on a discarded roll of barbed wire, and managed, thanks to my sandals, to imbed a sharp thorn in my foot.

"Crap!" I grumbled as I dropped the briefcase and bag, sat down in the wet grass, yanked off my sandal, and attempted to pull the thorn out.

"Lady, if I were you, I'd get the hell outta that pasture."

"Huh?" I looked up to see a young man, perhaps in his early twenties, leaning on the fence. He was wearing a baseball cap that sported the John Deere tractor logo, bib coveralls, and a sleeveless shirt. He was barefoot and had a shotgun draped over one arm. He stared at me with intensely blue eyes.

"I said I'd get outta that pasture if I were you." As he spoke he pointed behind me.

I turned. A large—no, make that a *huge*—Brahman bull was trotting purposefully in my direction.

"Holy crap!" I sprang up and turned to face the oncoming bull. He was perhaps thirty feet away, and he froze as soon as I stood, snorting and pawing the ground.

"Holy crap!" I repeated.

"Uh, lady? You'd best stop holy crappin' and get holy movin' if you know what's good for ya. Beelzebub don't take kindly to strangers on his turf. And unless you got a saltlick in that bag of yours, I suggest you make haste."

"Shit!" I grabbed my bag and briefcase and started for the fence.

"But whatever you do, don't run!"

The bull snorted again, sounding like a steam engine coming up behind me. I ran.

"No, I told you! Don't run!"

"Like hell!" I gasped, sprinting toward the fence. It was less than twenty feet away, but it felt like a mile. I had no idea whether or not Beelzebub was charging, and I wasn't about to turn around to find out.

About two feet from the fence my feet shot out from under me in the damp, slippery clay, and I went sprawling on my rear end. I screamed, expecting the raging bull to be on me at any moment. Scrambling to my feet, I dropped the bag, tore the briefcase off my shoulder, tossed it over the fence, and then clawed my way up after it. The top of the fence was barbed, but I didn't care. I teetered for a moment then tumbled. There was a jerk as my skirt caught on a barb, a loud tearing sound, and I landed with a resounding thump on the other side.

I opened my eyes to a pair of bare feet parked near my nose and lifted my gaze to find the young man crouched beside me. He was grinning.

"I told you not to run. It's downright slippery alongside the fence."

I sat up and wheeled around. Beelzebub had reached the bag of neonatal supplies I'd dropped and was pawing at them with a dinner plate-sized hoof.

"Shit!" I burst out.

"You sure do say 'shit' and 'crap' a lot." The young man held out his hand to help me up. I was covered in sticky red clay, had left one sandal behind in the pasture along with the bag of now-trampled neonatal supplies, and the backside of my skirt was ripped all the way to the waist. In addition, my foot throbbed thanks to the still-imbedded thorn.

"Shit, shit, SHIT," I repeated.

"I rest my case," he said. Taking my arm, he helped me hobble down the path to a small but tidy log cabin.

"I'm sorry," I gasped as I sank down on the porch steps. "I'm Kate Jacobs, with Child Protective Services."

"I know. The hospital called and told us you'd be headin' our way."

"You have a phone?" I asked, astonished. This was a rare thing in the hollers of Highton County.

"Of course." He held out his hand. "Will Thorpe," he said. "And this's my wife, Lee, and our son, Lil Will."

"Pleased to meet you," I managed as a slim woman with a swaddled newborn stepped through the front door.

Fifteen minutes later I was sitting in the Thorpes' spotless kitchen with my foot propped on a stool so Will could work out the thorn with his pocket knife. Lee had rinsed out my blouse and skirt and was sewing up the tear in the back. She had loaned me a pair of slacks and a T-shirt and poured me a glass of iced tea. I was holding the baby, who stared back at me with enormous blue eyes.

"There, that's done." Will slipped the knife back into his pocket and then took his son from my arms.

"Thank you!" I grinned at the young couple somewhat sheepishly.

"So the hospital's worried about Lil Will here, eh?" Will smiled down into his son's red, crumpled face. "Well, they don't need to worry. This lil guy here is well taken care of, ain't ya?" He kissed the baby on the nose.

Will was right. The baby was clearly well-fed, clean, and healthy. Lee told me he nursed lustily, had awakened twice during the night to feed, and then went right back to sleep. She was producing plenty of milk and thought mothering was "'bout the easiest thing in the world." And she made it look that way too.

Unlike most first-time parents, both she and Will held the baby comfortably, without that typical new-at-parenting awkwardness. The small cabin was tidy; they had a sturdy wooden crib and plenty of baby clothes; a load of crisp white diapers was hanging outside on a line, and both of them exuded an air of calm confidence in everything they did. Lee explained that she was the oldest of nine children and had been "raisin' young 'uns" as long as she could remember.

"The only thing what's bothered me is that Will wasn't at the birth," Lee told me sadly.

"Yep. Baby wasn't due for another three weeks, so I headed into town to pick up some hay and rabbit feed. Lil Will was here by the time I got to the hospital."

"Lil Will came so fast, I barely got myself to the hospital," Lee interjected.

"You drove yourself?" I asked, incredulous.

"Nope. Rode the mare down to Will's father's farm. They gave me a ride."

"You rode a horse while you were in labor?" I gasped.

"Beat walkin'," Lee answered with a shrug. "Your skirt's ready," she added. "Clothes are still a bit damp, but you can borrow mine. Just leave 'em at Sunrise Baptist Church in a bag with my name on 'em. We'll pick 'em up Sunday after service. Lessen you reckon you'll be comin' back here?"

"No, no need!" I smiled at her. "You three seem to be doing just fine—unless there's something you need help with?"

"Nope." Will put his arm around his wife. "We got everything we need right here."

I thanked them for their help, and they walked with me down the correct footpath that ran between the two pastures. Will then retrieved my missing sandal and gathered up what remained of the neonatal kit while Beelzebub looked on indifferently from beneath a shady tree. I stared at the destroyed neonatal scale. It wouldn't be the first loss I'd have to write up for Hilary.

Near the path was a large homemade hutch. While Will fetched my sandal, I leaned down to admire the long-eared rabbits inside.

"Will raises 'em. Won a couple of blue ribbons at the fair last year," Lee told me proudly.

When he returned, Will opened the hutch door and lifted up the black-and-white buck I had been petting. "Ya want one?" he asked. "Least we can do after Beelzebub scared you outta your shoes and skirt."

"I'd love one," I answered, thinking how much our little farm could use a pet. Peter and I were both gone from home too long to justify having a dog, but a rabbit would be perfect.

Will said, "Okay, I'll fix him right up." And with that he calmly and cleanly snapped the rabbit's neck. "You want me to gut him for ya too?"

My jaw dropped. "I—I didn't want to eat him!" I wailed. "I wanted him for a pet!"

Will stared at me in disbelief. "These here are eatin' rabbits. Who'd want a coney for a pet? They're food!"

I must have looked so horrified that he took pity on me. "No worries, ma'am. We'll cook him up ourselves." He squinted at me. "Ain't you never had rabbit stew?"

"Um, n-no," I managed, thanked them again, and took my leave as quickly as I could.

Later that afternoon I dropped a requisition for a new neonatal scale and a ten-dollar voucher for a rabbit on Hilary's desk. She eyed them carefully but didn't say a word.

When I went to the Baptist church the next day to drop off Lee Thorpe's clothes, the secretary smiled at me. "Lee phoned and told me you'd be droppin' off her things. She said to tell you thanks. Oh, and I'm supposed to invite you to the church prayer supper on Wednesday night. We're serving coney stew."

Of Courtroom Shenanigans and Liberace

The Devoe case was one I considered open and shut. Two girls, aged nine and twelve, had told their teacher that their uncle was molesting them. The forensic exam turned up evidence, and the parents were devastated that they had not adequately protected their daughters. They were cooperative, appropriate, and worked with me to ensure the girls received counseling and that the uncle would be prosecuted to the fullest extent of the law.

I had been subpoenaed into the initial informal fact-finding criminal court hearing to give a statement. Patrick went with me to represent CPS while Fred Hawkins, the prosecuting attorney, plopped himself down at our table.

I smiled a greeting when public defender Kay Thompson entered the courtroom and headed toward her table. I had worked with Kay on a number of cases and always found her to be fair and reasonable. Unlike some of the other defense attorneys, she often tried to reason with her clients and get them to work with, rather than against, their social worker. Kay and I had even gone out for drinks a few times, and although she was not a close friend, we did have a comfortable working relationship.

Thus I found it surprising that Kay rushed into the courtroom and sat down at the table without returning my smile or even looking at Patrick or me. She seemed irritated and uncomfortable, and I wondered what was wrong.

"All rise; Highton County Court is in session, the honorable Judge Nancy Morgan presiding," the bailiff intoned.

We rose as Judge Morgan, a sharp, no-nonsense woman, took her seat on the bench.

"Your Honor," the court clerk began, "you will be hearing the matter of the State versus Samuel P. Meggett."

I became aware that Kay was shifting uncomfortably in her chair. As I watched, she shuffled the papers in front of her, shuffled them again, sighed, and then pushed them away. Her client, who was sitting next to her, leaned over and whispered something in her ear. I saw her glare at him.

The judge picked up the file, read through it, then turned her attention to Kay. "Mrs. Thompson, how does your client plead?"

Kay stood up, her face bright red. "Your Honor," she said slowly, almost reluctantly, "my, um, my client has instructed me to plead not guilty on his behalf. He, er, that is, um, he wishes for the court to know that it is absolutely impossible for him to have sexually abused those girls. My client wishes for me to say"—here she coughed—"that he is the reincarnation of Liberace, and everyone knows that Liberace was gay and thus not interested in girls. Thank you, Your Honor." She sat down with a bump, her face the color of a ripe plum.

There were murmurs all around. Disbelieving laughter began to bubble inside me, and I bit my cheek to keep it from erupting. Beside me I could feel Patrick shaking. He pulled a tissue from his pocket and blew his nose noisily. Even the bailiff's lips were twitching. I didn't dare meet Patrick's eye; both of us were well aware that if we looked at each other we would dissolve into helpless snorts of laughter.

Kay Thompson sat rigid in her chair. She looked like she wanted to be anywhere else on earth than here in this courtroom.

I glanced up at the judge. How she managed to keep her face so utterly impassive was beyond me. The moment she caught my eye she quickly banged her gavel. "This court will take a five-minute recess," she ordered in a choked voice and rushed from the room.

The chamber door closed behind her, but not before we heard her shrieks of laughter.

Where Clueless Devils Tread

There have been many attempts to treat and rehabilitate sexual offenders. Unfortunately, "curing" a pedophile is akin to "curing" an alcoholic: it can't be done. Offenders can learn to control their behavior, but the desire remains.

Rape is often called a crime of violence because the perpetrator seeks to harm his victim. In child sexual assault, the offender is quite simply sexually aroused by children. Incidentally, "he" is the correct gender choice to describe the typical sexual offender as 97 percent of all sexual offenders are male. And in 93 percent of cases the child knows the offender. Most are family acquaintances, with about half being actual family members. Fathers, stepfathers, a mother's boyfriend, uncles, and brothers all contend for top offender places.[2]

Additionally, and contrary to misconception, gay and lesbian men and women rarely, if ever, sexually abuse children. The arousal a male pedophile exhibits toward boys is not homosexual in nature. It is pedophilia. The simple fact is that child sexual offenders are in love with children. They work hard to ingratiate themselves into their victims' and their victims' families' favors. Once they have successfully begun abusing the child, they buy the child's silence through the promise of gifts and favors or threats of harm or other repercussions.

One thing is certain: abuse is NEVER the fault of the child, no matter what.

I was once asked to sit in on a group session for child sexual offenders so that I could share with these men the impact their criminal actions had on their victims and their victims' families. I remember wondering why these men even had to have this "impact" pointed out to them. *Of course* these men must know what harm they'd done. Wasn't that a given?

Oh, how naïve I was back then!

The first thing that struck me about this offender group was what good-looking men they were. I remember as a grade-school child being repeatedly shown the safety film *The Dangerous Stranger*, which featured a sleazy-looking, unshaven man attempting to lure a little girl into his car. The men sitting in this meeting were anything but sleazy and unshaven. They ranged in ages from their early twenties to their seventies; they were nicely dressed and well groomed, and many of them were even handsome.

What also struck me about them was how polite they were.

The session leaders had previously explained to me that this is exactly how many perpetrators win over their victims and garner the denial of other adults: simply by being some of the nicest and friendliest guys on earth.

The "Dangerous Stranger" really isn't a stranger, and the film's title is definitely a misnomer. *The Dangerous Coach, Scout Leader, Sunday School Teacher, Priest, Rabbi*...whatever...would be a far more accurate description. And while the vast majority of coaches, scout leaders, Sunday school teachers, priests, rabbis, and others are certainly not sex offenders, pedophiles easily fit into and hide in these roles, which allows them ready access to children.

The men were asked to introduce themselves and briefly relate their offenses. I nodded to each of them in turn as they stated their names and what they'd done, and I learned another thing right away: sexual offenders cannot be "categorized."

The range of offenses they calmly described for me was shocking. I didn't know how to react other than to sit there and continue nodding in greeting. I realized that not one of them fit any single category of abuser. That is, whether they were called rapists, pedophiles, "Peeping Toms," or whatever else, these men were all, quite simply, addicted to sex—of any kind.

What this basically amounts to is that while some of these offenders might be aroused by children and others by violence, if they can't ensnare their preferred victim or deviancy of choice, they will go for whatever they can get. So, for example, if a sexual offender is unable to "get" his preferred prepubescent girl, he will "settle" for a teenage boy.

Unfortunately, a sexual offender's actions are generally, and usually innocently, aided by other adults. Consider: An offense as damaging as the abuse itself can come from otherwise well-meaning people such as the members of Amanda's fundamentalist church. By defending the abuser and accusing Amanda of lying, they themselves became part of the victimization and were as guilty of the abuse as Amanda's stepfather.

Years later, after leaving frontline CPS social work and becoming a social work educator, an exercise I used to conduct in my classes was to have participants think about a close relative, friend, or community leader, and then describe how they would respond if this individual were to be accused of child sexual assault.

Across the board the answer was always, "No way! He'd *never* do such a thing!" And this image—of being beyond the capability of harming a child—is what offenders work very hard to portray.

At the end of our meeting, the offenders were encouraged to ask me questions. The first one was, "Oh, come on. Have we really hurt these kids?"

My initial response was speechlessness. I realized at that moment just how skewed reality was for these men. They honestly believed that they had not done any harm to their victims, and after more questioning, it became clear to me that some even believed that their victims had welcomed their advances.

I recall having once been shown photos that sexual deviancy therapists use to determine whether or not a client is sexually deviant. One such photo showed a toddler standing in diapers with her arms outstretched.

To a healthy adult, the photo translates to the toddler wanting to be picked up. To a sexually deviant pedophile, the toddler is saying "I want it," with *it* being sexual advances. Offensive, yes, but this is the harsh reality of pedophiles. They are turned on by kids. And more times than not, they're the least likely people to arouse suspicion.

When a Mother's Heart Is Torn

Breanne Kimmer gave birth to her daughter and then gave her away. It was not a legal adoption; in fact, no one knew that she was even pregnant. Sixteen, scared, the daughter of a strict fundamentalist minister, Breanne managed to hide her swelling belly under baggy pants and a sweatshirt. When the time of her confinement approached, Breanne convinced her mother that she wanted to go to Atlanta for a revival, but her real intention was to hide in a local hostel, have the baby, and leave it somewhere—anywhere. After that she would go home, and her parents would never know. To Breanne's immense relief, her parents allowed her to go to the revival and arranged for her to stay in a hostel run by a local church.

When she got to the hostel, the kind receptionist took one look at Breanne and asked her, "When is your baby due?"

Terrified, Breanne broke down in tears and begged the woman not to disclose her secret.

"I think I can help you," Elvira Clark, the receptionist, told her. She invited Breanne to dinner at her home and introduced her to her brother and his wife, Don and Mary Wheaton, who had also been invited. They had a lovely dinner, and Elvira suggested to Breanne that she stay with her and her husband rather than in the hostel. Breanne readily agreed.

Elvira called Breanne's mother to make the arrangements and suggested that Breanne stay a bit longer—that they would enjoy hiring Breanne to work with their church's summer camp. Breanne's parents, ignorant of the real situation, agreed to this as well.

The next night the Wheatons returned to Elvira's house. They admitted to Breanne that Elvira had invited them to dinner solely to meet her and that the couple had been trying unsuccessfully for years to conceive.

"Would you maybe consider giving us your baby?" Mary asked.

Breanne stared at the Wheatons in wonder. This was the answer to her prayers! The Wheatons misinterpreted her astonished look as fear and reassured her that no one ever need know. They would not go through an adoption agency, Breanne could just have the baby in the Clarks' home, and then she could leave without it. They would take care of everything else. Only Breanne had to promise that she would never try to see the baby.

Relieved beyond belief, Breanne agreed.

Breanne went into labor eleven days later. The baby was a beautiful, healthy little girl, and Breanne made the mistake of holding her. That's when Breanne Kimmer fell in love with her daughter. But Breanne also realized that she could never bring the baby home, knowing her father would beat her within an inch of her life. He had threatened her with this many times whenever he thought she was "going astray" with a boy. Her parents had no idea she even had a boyfriend, and she had never told the baby's father that she was pregnant.

The Wheatons and the Clarks remained kind but firm and convinced Breanne she was doing the right thing by leaving her baby with them. Tearfully Breanne agreed, and a week later she returned home without her child. Her secret was safe; her parents would never know about her pregnancy—or so she thought.

***

Two years went by. Two years during which Breanne never stopped thinking about her baby. She wondered where she was, how she looked, and what she was doing. She dreamed about her, thought about her, and wished she had never, ever given her up. She lost weight, she grew increasingly depressed, and her worried parents took the now eighteen-year-old girl to a psychiatrist. There, the whole story came out.

To Breanne's surprise her parents were not angry that she had gotten pregnant; however, they were furious that she had not told them and had given the baby—their granddaughter—away. When they learned the adoption had not been legal, they made a simple decision. They were going to get the baby back.

And so began a series of heartbreaking legal events. The baby's father was dragged into the situation, suits and countersuits were launched, and in the end, to the dismay of almost everyone in the courtroom, the little girl was awarded back to Breanne.

The child had known no other mother than Mary Wheaton. To the child, Breanne Kimmer was a complete and utter stranger. In the infinite wisdom of the courts, it was determined that a sudden, abrupt, and complete separation from the people she knew as her parents would be in the best interest of the child.

Those of us following the case in the news were horrified. The Wheatons were ordered to bring the child to Highton County Courthouse. A social worker and detective were ordered to make the "transfer" there. Not one of us was willing to do so. Hilary had us draw straws. I lost.

The Wheatons stood in the courtroom desperately clutching the toddler they had named Erin. They begged Judge Dawley not to make them go through with this, they pleaded, they cried. Breanne Kimmer stood in the back of the courtroom with her parents.

The judge motioned for me to take the child. A higher state court had already decided; this was not his decision to make, but it was his order to carry out.

I couldn't. I stood rooted to the spot.

"NOW, Mrs. Jacobs, or I'll have you arrested for contempt of court."

I moved forward robotically. Mary Wheaton was sobbing. I pulled the toddler from her mother's arms, and the little girl began to scream.

"Mommy! Mommy! Mommy!"

My heart broke, and tears streamed down my face. I felt like a monster.

"Mommmmmmeeeeeeee!" Erin screamed.

I all but threw her into Breanne Kimmer's arms and then ran from the courtroom. I didn't stop until I reached the culvert where the creek spilled into the courthouse park. I sank down beside the water and burst into tears. I cried and cried. I cried for Mary Wheaton, I cried for Erin, I cried for every kid I had ever interviewed and placed in foster care. I cried because my marriage was failing, because I felt helpless and hopeless and didn't know where to turn.

A shadow fell over me, and suddenly Nona Davies settled her huge bulk beside me. To this day I have no idea where she came from. She just wrapped her enormous arm around my shoulder and I buried my face against her and sobbed.

Of Endings and Beginnings

Dilly and Beth were expecting!

They made the big announcement on the Fourth of July while the "Chaos Troop," as the six of us called ourselves—meaning Dilly and Beth, Virginia and Stephan, and Peter and me—was once again cruising around the lake on Dilly's houseboat.

We had anchored in a cove, which offered a good vantage spot for watching the fireworks that would be set off later from the marina. We'd spent the better part of the day swimming, sunning, stuffing ourselves on hotdogs, chips, and other glorious junk food, and were now lazing on the upper deck of the houseboat.

I was sunburned and content to lie there lazily dropping popcorn into the dark green water to watch the fish snap it up. Peter climbed up to the roof with a bucket of ice-cold beer, which he began passing around.

Beth was lying with her head on Dilly's lap, and she waved away the bottle he offered her.

"What?" Peter asked. "Miss Malt and Hops herself passing up on a brew? And not just any brew, mind you—an ice-cold Heineken! For real?"

Beth shook her head. "Pass."

Dilly grabbed the one Peter handed him, flipped off the lid, then untangled himself from Beth and stood up. He banged a knife on the side of the bottle for attention.

"Hear ye, hear ye, hear ye!" he intoned. "The lovely, the very lovely Mrs.

Dillon Bracks and I have an announcement to make!"

We looked up expectantly as Beth stood and Dilly wrapped his arm around her.

"The members of the Chaos Troop are going to increase by one sometime in February. Let us toast to the arrival of our son!"

"Or daughter," Beth added, grinning like a fool and socking her husband on the arm.

"A baby? You two are going to have a baby? Oh, Beth! How wonderful!" I pulled her into a hug and the two of us began jumping up and down like silly school kids.

For a few moments there was pandemonium on the upper deck. Stephan was pumping Dilly's hand, Peter pulled Beth into a bear hug and was spinning her around, I was laughing and telling Peter to be careful—he was manhandling a pregnant woman—while Virginia was trying to hug the spinning Beth. It was a happy, tumultuous hullaballoo.

What a contrast, I thought later as we settled back on deck chairs to watch the fireworks explode over the trees. *A wonderful, happily married, and settled couple that very much want a baby. If I could make any wish, it would be that every child in the world could start out just like this.*

***

Dilly and I were on shift together a few weeks later when we were toned out to a place known to the locals as Slim Pickens Holler. (Toning out was the then-current system of alerting local fire departments to a call. Prior to the days of cell phones or the Internet, different sounding "tones" would be sent out over the fire departments' radios and pagers. Each department knew the sound of its own tones. After the tone, a brief description of the call, such as "MVA" [motor vehicle accident] or "ill female" would be followed by the address.)

In this case both Dilly and I knew the address well because we'd been there several times already. This hollow, or holler, was the home of Laura Mae Dicks and her great-grandmother, Pearl Ann. Laura Mae was seventeen years old. She had been born in the holler to Pearl Ann's granddaughter, Theresa.

Theresa had begun drinking heavily before she was fifteen, had gotten pregnant at seventeen, and delivered a premature Laura Mae at home. The midwife hadn't arrived in time, and Pearl Ann had delivered the tiny infant herself. The cord had been firmly wrapped around the baby's neck, and she was born blue. The midwife had arrived at just that moment and immediately began resuscitating the infant.

Her efforts had succeeded, but she had confided to Pearl Ann later that she wished they hadn't. Laura Mae suffered from fetal alcohol syndrome, hydrocephaly, and cerebral palsy on top of the post-birth anoxia and prematurity. She also had spina bifida and was blind.

Theresa took one look at her daughter and left the holler for good. It was up to Pearl Ann to care for Laura Mae. The midwife tried to convince her to send her great-granddaughter to a nursing facility to be cared for, but Pearl Ann refused. Numerous visits to the hospital and the gentle suggestions of the hospital staff and social workers yielded the same result.

"She ain't gonna live long—y'all have told me that," Pearl Ann always said. "She's had her surgery to close up her back, and that's all I'm gonna subject this baby to. She's my great-grand, and I'm takin' her home to live amongst her kin. And that's that."

Pearl Ann Dicks bundled up her great-granddaughter and brought her home to the holler.

Periodically, home-health nurses would check in on the two of them, and they had to admit that Pearl Ann was doing the best job with Laura Mae that anyone possibly could. Pearl Ann doted on her tiny great-granddaughter. She fed and bathed her, exercised her tiny limbs, sang to her, and told her stories.

To everyone's surprise, Laura Mae lived beyond her first birthday, then her second and her third, her fifth…

***

When Laura Mae turned fifteen, a hospital bed was brought up to the holler, and home-health nurses increased their visits to twice a week since the aging Pearl Ann simply could not handle the girl's physical care by herself anymore. By sixteen Laura Mae was contractured and completely bedridden, but she appeared to be happy and would coo and gurgle when her great-grandmother sang to her.

Avery Jessup, the minister of Nona's AME church, arranged to have members of his nearby parish visit Laura Mae and Pearl Ann regularly, and it was Reverend Jessup who called for an ambulance to come take Laura Mae to the hospital. Pearl Ann had died that morning, alone in her bed, and now there was no one to take care of the severely handicapped girl.

Slim Pickens Holler was one of the most remote and inaccessible "gaps" in Highton County. There was no road up to it, only a rugged mountain path that forded several streams and that tended to wash out the trail every spring. The visiting nurses and the rural physician, Dr. Hannah Driscoll, would either hike in the two miles to the homestead or Dr. Driscoll would ride in on horseback. The small house, hand-hewn by Pearl Ann's father and expanded by her husband, was almost one hundred years old, and heading into the holler truly felt like stepping back in time.

When the call came, Dilly and I drove the rig as far up the road as we could, then with the help of other members of the mountain rescue team, we hauled the Stokes litter up the trail for Laura Mae. To our surprise, Reverend Jessup was sitting by Laura Mae's bedside when we arrived, and Dr. Driscoll was pulling a stethoscope from around her neck.

"Laura Mae's gone too," she said quietly.

Dilly and I looked at each other. There was no medical reason for Laura Mae's death. True, she had lived many years longer than anyone expected, but was her passing on the same day as Pearl Ann's coincidental? (Though the death certificate would later list the cause of death as complications from cystic fibrosis, I've always wondered if maybe they just wanted to go together.)

Now I turned away and saw that Pearl Ann's body had been laid out in the front bedroom, the requisite silver coins on her eyes and a clutch of honeysuckle tucked in her weathered hands.

The house was, as always, immaculate. The wooden floor was polished, and beautiful hand-hooked rugs added splashes of color, as did the bright quilts lovingly made by Pearl Ann.

Outside, Pearl Ann's extensive garden was bursting with corn, squash, kale, peas, carrots, lettuce, and young pumpkins. Bees buzzed noisily around the small orchard of apples, pears, and peaches.

Inside the kitchen, Pearl Ann's pantry was filled with put-up jams, beans, headcheese, beets, and other colorful produce. Pearl Ann Dicks, I realized as I looked around me, had provided her severely handicapped great-granddaughter with everything she could have ever wanted or needed.

Dilly turned to Dr. Driscoll. "I guess we'll have to haul both bodies out of here. Can't leave them much longer in this heat."

"No need," Reverend Jessup said. "We'll just bury them up here in the family plot."

We all nodded our agreement.

With the help of the EMTs, it didn't take long to dig one large grave. Dr. Driscoll radioed down to dispatch and was relayed through to the coroner's office. He gave Dr. Driscoll the order to sign the death certificates and go ahead and bury the two women. Pearl Ann and Laura Mae Dicks were laid to rest, side by side, on the shoulder of Slim Pickens Holler's looming mountain.

It was late when the dozen or so of us trooped back down the trail by the light of our headlamps. Before climbing back into the rig, I looked up one last time at the mountain that had been the home of the Dicks family for over a hundred years.

"You all right, Miss Kate?"

I turned to find Reverend Jessup standing beside me.

"Yeah, Reverend, I am. I was just thinking that even though they were two of the poorest people in the world, they were probably the richest."

"Amen to that," he said softly. "Amen to that."

When the Pendulum Swings

Unfortunately, child abuse and neglect have been a part of human existence almost since our species appeared on this planet. In some cultures the misuse of children was accepted as a norm. Ancient Romans treated the underclass or orphaned children as sexual toys; only children of the wealthy upper class were considered untouchable and recognized in public by the jewelry they wore. Infanticide existed in many cultures, and although typically frowned upon, it was often ignored.

In some middle-eastern cultures, fathers put their unmarried daughters to death for disobeying or dishonoring a family by being seen in the company of an unrelated male. Even today genital mutilation is still performed in some cultures as a method to ensure a woman's fidelity to her husband. Child labor laws in this country were not passed until the early 1900s, and in rural Appalachia, children were sometimes put to work in coalmines, laboring for little or no pay in unsafe and abysmal conditions.

Until recently, domestic violence was considered "a private matter" across most of America. I can remember as a child in the 1960s going for evening walks with my father through our quiet, middle-class neighborhood and hearing shouting, screams, and the sound of breaking glass coming from a neighbor's house. The children who lived there often appeared in school with cuts and bruises, which they typically explained away as "sports injuries." Abuse was not talked about; it was nobody's business, and most of society pretended it didn't exist.

It was not until 1875 that the first organization devoted entirely to child protection came into existence in the United States: the New York Society for the Prevention of Cruelty to Children. By 1922, there were approximately three hundred non-governmental child protection societies scattered across the country, although many cities and almost all rural areas had no access to this type of service.[3]

In 1935, the newly established Social Security Act contained an obscure provision that called for "the protection and care of homeless, dependent, and neglected children and children in danger of becoming delinquent."[4]

In 1956, Vincent De Francis, director of the Children's Division of the American Humane Association, conducted a nationwide inventory of Child Protection Services and found only eighty-four non-governmental services in the United States, down from an earlier three hundred-plus at the turn of the century.

A subsequent survey by De Francis in 1967 showed that the number of such agencies had dwindled to less than ten. By then nearly all states had placed child protection into the government's hands, but many states did not have agencies specializing in child protection.[5]

In 1962, Edward Kempe wrote in a *Newsweek* article:

One day last November we had four battered children in our pediatric ward. Two died in the hospital, one died at home four weeks later. For every child who enters the hospital this badly beaten, there must be hundreds treated by unsuspecting doctors. The battered child syndrome isn't a reported disease, but it damn well ought to be.[6]

By 1967, all states had passed Child Abuse and Neglect reporting laws. By 1974, sixty thousand cases were reported; by 1990, two million; by 2000, over three million cases were reported. As late as 1974, then U.S. Senator Walter Mondale wrote: *Nowhere in the federal government could we find even one official assigned full time to the prevention, identification, and treatment of child abuse and neglect.*[7]

It was not until 1970 that the topic of child sexual assault was broached publicly and introduced into the spectrum of child abuse and neglect laws.[8]

Sadly the war on child abuse and neglect is nowhere near being won.

According to the American Society for the Prevention of Cruelty to Children, the 2015 Child Maltreatment Report calls child abuse a "hidden epidemic" that is "grossly under-reported."[9] The 2017 version of the report shows an increase from 3.6 million to 4 million CPS intakes in the past two years, representing approximately 7.4 million children in the United States alone.[10]

During my time in Highton County, the pendulum of abuse was clearly swinging in a new direction of acknowledging the problem as opposed to denying it, along with the grudging acceptance of legal intervention into what was once considered "a private family matter." Unfortunately from my perspective as a Child Protective Services caseworker in the mountains of North Carolina, I often found myself wondering if the pendulum was swinging too far. The story of Edwin "Bull" Daniels was a case in point.

Edwin Daniels was born the first of seven children to a North Carolina tobacco farmer. Everyone expected him to follow in his daddy's footsteps, and when Edwin turned ten, he began to work the fields alongside his father. His parents demanded that he finish school before he took over the farm as his father was adamant that Edwin learn how to keep the books properly. As a farmhand, Edwin watched a slew of migrant workers come and go, their children often completely unschooled, forced to work the fields, and often abused by the foreman or even their own parents.

By sixteen, Edwin had grown into a huge young man. At six feet four inches, he towered over other boys his age and weighed in at well over two hundred pounds, earning him the nickname "Bull."

When he was eighteen years old, Bull happened to arrive at a neighboring farm just as the father of a migrant child picked up the boy, threw him against an electric fence, and then began to beat him with his fists. Bull didn't think twice. He reached them in two strides, grabbed the father by the collar, slapped him, and threatened to kill him if he ever laid hands on a child again. He then carried the boy across the field to his father's pickup truck and drove him to the hospital.

From that day on, Edwin "Bull" Daniels vowed to watch over all the children he could.

At age twenty-six, Bull married, but the couple was unable to have children of their own. Instead they fostered and adopted a number of "young 'uns."

The year he turned forty, Bull's wife died of cancer, leaving him alone on the farm. By now Bull had come to realize the enormous health risks of smoking tobacco, and he decided that he no longer wanted to farm such a "disreputable" product. He shut down the farm and turned it into a foster group-home.

Bull asked that only children over the age of eight be placed with him, preferably boys. It wasn't that he was prejudiced toward girls or babies, but he felt that women did a better job of raising "young 'uns" in their early years. Thus he took in many hard-to-place, troubled male teens and turned them around through excellent role modeling, hard work, and self-esteem-enhancing activities such as horseback riding, hiking, and rock climbing.

Bull Daniels was an outstanding foster parent, a true mentor to troubled young boys, and a godsend to the courts and social workers of Highton and the surrounding counties.

One evening an on-call social worker phoned Bull. She had a desperate situation: a sibling group, two girls and a boy ages three, six, and eleven, had been removed from their home when their father had beaten their mother almost to death. The children were shell-shocked, and the social worker feared that separating them into different foster homes would traumatize them even more.

Bull reluctantly agreed to take them on.

After the children had been with Bull for almost a week, he realized that the youngest, three-year-old Darla, had not had a bath since her arrival. So Bull did what any responsible parent would do: he filled the tub, tossed in some bath toys and bubble bath, and helped Darla clean herself up. He gently scrubbed her hair, washed her from head to toe, dried her off, and slipped her into clean pajamas. He also helped her with her toileting.

Unfortunately, those simple gestures of good parenting were Bull's undoing. Little Darla told her older brother that Bull had "touched her on the pee-pee."

A Child Protective Services investigation was launched. Bull was found innocent, but the experience forever changed the way Bull was able to parent.

Bull was known as an affectionate man who greeted social workers with hugs, who taught troubled teenage boys that it was not just all right but "manly" to accept embraces and show affection, who frequently gave children piggyback rides or took the boys skinny-dipping in the creek that ran through his farm. He never raised a hand to a child; rather, he disciplined them through understanding, firmness, and kindness.

From the day of the allegation on, Bull Daniels stopped hugging his kids—children who probably needed healthy, safe touching more than anyone. Where he had always found one-on-one time for each of his charges, he never again placed himself in any situation where he would be alone with a child.

The much-loved skinny-dips in the creek stopped, as did the piggyback rides, and Bull turned from a warm-hearted, jovial man into one who was quiet and reserved. Ultimately he gave up foster parenting altogether.

***

Bull Daniels is an example of the pendulum of child protection swinging too far. In schools across America, teachers were suddenly being warned not to physically touch or, heaven forbid, hug their students. The hyper-fear of sexual abuse charges became the undoing not only of a good man like Bull Daniels but countless other foster parents just like him.

Often when I spoke with groups about becoming foster parents, the response was "Hell, no! Why would we willingly expose ourselves to the possibility of being accused of molesting a child?"

The foster care system suffered. Foster parents are still desperately needed throughout the United States, and the very rare instance of an abusive foster parent aside, most are truly among the most loving, dedicated humans on this planet.

Sadly, the world still needs men like Bull Daniels.

Of Parenting and Iced Tea

Without question, the time when new parents feel the most overwhelmed and the chance of accidents or serious problems arising is greatest when they bring a newborn home from the hospital. Exhausted, unskilled parents, a fussy or screaming baby, lack of sleep, and a sense of being overwhelmed can do in even the most well-meaning moms and dads.

For this reason, in the 1970s and 1980s, many hospitals throughout the United States developed postpartal (after birth) parenting programs. Classes on everything from baby care to breastfeeding were offered in hospitals, and home-health nurses made routine visits to all first-time mothers, regardless of their social class or level of education. (I received such a visit after my first daughter was born, and at first I insisted that as an RN and EMT I did not need such an intervention. When the home-health nurse came out, however, I found her to be a wealth of information and support.) Unfortunately, by the turn of the century, most hospitals had to do away with the home-health nursing programs due to budget cuts. This was a terrible loss for all new parents and their infants

Kim Andrews, by all appearances, was a rock-solid, calm, and level-headed new mother. She had only a tenth-grade education and no family nearby, so the hospital decided to ask CPS to conduct a welfare check on her about a week after her baby was born. Because of my nursing background, Hilary asked if I would make the call, which I did gladly. Kim lived in a small but neat trailer not far out of town. She had a well-tended garden, was receiving

AFDC and food stamps, and seemed to be handling motherhood well. I weighed and measured her baby, an adorable little boy named Michael.

But at one week old, I discovered that Michael had lost considerable weight since birth. While almost all newborns drop some weight immediately after birth, a healthy baby will regain this weight within a few days and begin steadily increasing in size. But Michael was doing the opposite.

Before I could begin to question Kim about how nursing was going, she stood up and pulled a bottle containing a clear brown liquid out of the refrigerator. She held this under hot water to warm it up then stuck the bottle in Michael's mouth. He sucked lustily.

"Kim," I asked, "what are you feeding him?"

"Iced tea."

My jaw dropped. "Kim, he needs to have either breast milk or formula!"

"Oh, I know that," Kim said casually. "But he fussed so much over the breast that he just lay there screaming and hollering. Breastfeeding just didn't work for us. I was drinking iced tea and poured a little in his mouth, and he liked it. So I feed it to him."

I was aghast. I tried in vain to explain that breast milk and formula were food, not "drink" to a baby and that iced tea offered no nutrition for him whatsoever, but Kim would not be deterred.

I arranged for a home-health nurse to make routine visits to Kim's place and opened a neglect case on the family. Once she received support and education, Kim became a model mother. The situation left me wondering, however, how many other Kims were out there, endangering their newborns' growth and development through simple ignorance. A reduction in the home-health program might have saved dollars up front, but in the end, it was costing counties far more in interventive care.

Of Comings and Goings

Tammy Adams was a beautiful, sweet-natured college student with waist-length blond hair and brilliant green eyes. I met her one summer when she enrolled in a basic climbing class that Beth, Dilly, and I were teaching.

Tammy and her mother lived on one of the more populated hilltops in Highton. Tammy had been raised by her mother, who had encouraged the girl to make more out of her life in terms of education and career choices than she herself had. Tammy was so sweet, bubbly, and beautiful that it was not surprising that every male in our class fell in love with her.

She began dating one of the younger EMTs, and as bad luck—or more likely poor planning—would have it, the couple ended up pregnant. When Tammy told her boyfriend, he told her he was not ready to be a parent, gave her money for an abortion, and vanished from her life.

Tammy's mother rallied around her daughter and promised to help raise her grandchild if Tammy would agree to finish college after the baby was born. Tammy agreed and asked me if I would act as her labor coach. I told her I would be honored.

Also living in the area, just above the Adams's home, was the Green family. Old Ida Green was one of the true matriarchs of Highton County. At the age of 102 she still went to church regularly and frequented the local restaurants and diners, where she would give the cooks a "talkin' to" if the food was not up to her impeccable standards.

Ida herself was a great cook. She was sharp as a tack, never missed the local music festival, and still played the dulcimer beautifully. Everyone in town affectionately referred to her as Grandma Green. Grandma loved living, but she made it clear that she was tired and ready for the "man upstairs" to take her home.

"He must have forgotten me," she would often say with a sigh. I came to hear this statement frequently when Peter and I visited the Greens. We had befriended Grandma's great-grandson, Everett, and as a result were often invited to dinner.

The Greens lived in a rambling log house that had started out as a small cabin. Every generation of Green men had added to it, and although it was beautiful and well kept, the numerous additions made it one of the oddest-shaped homes imaginable. It perched on top of a holler ridge and had a huge deck that jutted out over the valley. A long, winding stairwell connected the house to the much lower garage, and a short path connected the garage to the home of Tammy and her mother.

Tammy Adams went into labor on a cold, clear November night. That same night "the man upstairs" must have finally remembered Grandma Green and decided to summon her home. Everett called me to tell me his great-grandmother was ailing about five minutes after Tammy had phoned to tell me that she was having contractions.

Highton boasted a small rural hospital that was only twenty minutes down the highway from Tammy's home, so I wasn't too worried about getting Tammy there in a hurry. I told her I would stop by and check on her shortly; hopefully she would be able to labor at home for a while.

When Everett Green phoned a few minutes later and asked me to come see his great-grandmother, I quickly agreed. Being as they lived so close together, I knew I could "kill two birds with one stone" as it were.

Most of the older generations of mountain folk were born and died in their own homes. To mountain families, death was an accepted part of life, and it wasn't uncommon for an entire family to gather around the bed to "celebrate" as a loved one passed. Everett Green and his wife, Frances, were alone with Grandma, however, and he admitted to being somewhat unnerved by the process of death. He wanted to call for an ambulance, but his wife argued that Grandma would never have cottoned to that.

When I arrived at the Greens' just a few minutes later, I found Grandma unconscious and in Cheyne-Stokes respirations, a series of rapidly increasing breaths followed by a deep sigh. I knew the end was near.

Everett only needed a bit of reassurance that what was happening was normal and that his beloved great-grandmother was not suffering. I sat with the Greens for a while, gave them some instructions, then kissed Grandma good-bye on the forehead and made my way down the long, hand-hewn stairs and across the dirt path to Tammy's home.

Tammy was still relatively comfortable, her contractions were over ten minutes apart, her water had not broken, and she was barely three centimeters dilated. I reassured her that her baby's birth was still hours away and we had plenty of time to get to the hospital, or else we could go now if she wished.

She conferred with her mother, and the two of them decided that Tammy would be more comfortable remaining at home as long as she could. Leaving Tammy in her mother's care, I headed out to my car to grab a book and my pillow so I could get some rest during what would no doubt be a long, tiring night.

My car was parked in a clearing alongside the log-hewn garage. It was cold and crisp, and the stars shone brilliantly above the bare trees.

As I stood outside and looked up, I felt awed and humbled to be a part of something so large and so beautiful. In the home above me a wonderful old woman lay dying, more than ready to return to her true home and her maker; in the home below me a woman lay laboring to bring another life into the world.

I smiled and said a quiet prayer of gratitude.

It's Not Brotherly Love—It's Abuse

The Marsh family came screaming into my life late one night when I was covering an EMT shift at the fire station for someone who had called in sick. Peter hated it when I spent nights at the station, but he was in Chicago on business, so I hadn't hesitated when Dilly called and asked if I'd come in.

Most nights at the Highton Fire Department were quiet, and they paid us volunteers a small stipend whenever we worked a full eight hours at the station. Dilly was on duty with me, and Beth joined us for a few hours then headed home to bed. She was almost eight months pregnant and more than ready to have her baby. Dilly reluctantly saw her to her car, and then the two of us turned into our respective dorms and fell asleep.

We were awakened by dispatch tones shortly after midnight for a call that was toned out as "major laceration with heavy bleeding."

We arrived at the address, a run-down trailer on the outskirts of town, and were met at the top of the driveway by a hysterical woman. We could hear screaming as we grabbed the kits from the rig.

The woman shepherded us into the trailer and down the hall into a tiny bedroom where a gruesome sight met our eyes. A boy of perhaps seventeen lay on the bed, naked. He was covered in blood from his knees to his waist and was hanging onto his penis, or, rather, what was left of it.

He was shrieking in agony and simultaneously shouting obscenities at the teenage girl who was standing in the doorway. She was holding a bloody knife in her hands and looked at us defiantly. "Drop the knife, sweetheart," Dilly ordered firmly while I quickly radioed for police backup.

The girl dropped the knife, and Dilly kicked it far under the bed. "Sit," he barked at her, "in that chair, and don't move a muscle." She sat obediently in the chair, folded her arms, and glared at the boy on the bed.

"You fucking bitch!" he shrieked. "I'm going to fucking kill you! I'm going to kill you! You hear me?"

"Not if'n I kill you first," she hissed back, "which I about did."

Oh Lord, I groaned inwardly, *domestic violence at its worst*.

A deputy sheriff pushed his way into the small room. Dilly had already stuffed gauze against the boy's genitals and was applying pressure to the wound.

"You hurt?" I asked the girl. She shook her head no.

"Did you do this?" the deputy barked at her.

She nodded yes, and tears began to stream down her face. The deputy grabbed her and led her from the room.

Dilly and I continued to stanch the bleeding and stabilize the boy. As we were carrying him across the yard to the rig, I saw the girl sitting in the back of the squad car.

I helped Dilly load the gurney into the ambulance, and while he started an IV, I went over to the police car. The officer was one I had worked with on CPS cases, and I asked if I could talk with the girl.

"She won't need placement tonight, Miz Jacobs," he said. "I'm taking her to JuVee."

JuVee, or juvenile hall, was where minors who had been charged with a crime were taken. The teens' mother was arguing with the officer, telling him that it wasn't the girl's fault and he should leave her alone.

With the officer's permission, I opened the squad car door and crouched down to talk with the sobbing, handcuffed girl.

Her name was Lila. She told me that her brother had been sexually assaulting her for years, threatening to kill her if she told their mother. That night her brother had forced her not only to go down on him, but on several of his friends as well. Believing his threats of killing her if she didn't obey, Lila had complied.

Later, when her brother's friends had left and he had fallen asleep, Lila had crept into his room with a knife and attempted to castrate him. The knife had sliced deep into his groin and almost halfway through his penis.

I let Lila talk, showing only encouragement and sympathy as the terrible tale spilled from her, nearly every word she spoke punctuated by sobs.

"I couldn't take it no more," she finally whispered between hiccoughs, "I couldn't take it no more! First my daddy, then him, and now his friends..." Lila's voice trailed off as she buried her face in her cuffed hands and sobbed.

I urged the deputy to take her to the county hospital. To my relief, he agreed. Lila's brother would be transported all the way to Asheville as his wounds were more than the local hospital could handle.

Although the deputy kept Lila under arrest when he drove off in his patrol car, he simultaneously took her into protective custody. Eventually the case was turned over to a permanency planning worker, but I was called in to testify both in criminal court and family court.

Judge John Dawley heard the family case, and for once he did not argue against the caseworker's recommendations. His face actually blanched when he saw the photos of the boy's mutilated genitals. In no uncertain terms he ordered that all social worker recommendations be followed.

It turned out later that the Marsh family had come to the attention of Child Protective Services earlier in a neighboring county for allegations of sexual assault against Lila's father and brother for abusing Lila.

Lila's father had been sentenced to two years in jail. The case against Lila's brother had been taken before a family court judge, and despite physical evidence and clear testimony on the part of Lila Marsh that she was being sexually abused by her brother, the judge went against the social worker's recommendation and sent the girl back home. That judge had been the Honorable John Dawley.

Another Bald-Headed Baby

The last day in January surprised us all with an ice storm. The temperature had dropped so fast and so suddenly that the rain that had been falling earlier in the day turned to ice. The power lines snapped, trees exploded as their sap froze, huge branches broke off and sent even more power lines hurtling to the ground. The roads turned into sheets of glistening black ice, and everything in Highton County ground to a standstill.

Virginia and I had been at Dilly and Beth's when the storm hit, preparing for their baby shower later in the day. Beth was enormously pregnant and feeling very uncomfortable. She slept while Virginia and I decorated the living room, made sandwiches and punch, and iced the cake. The party was due to begin at two, but by noon the sky was black and the storm had begun. By one o'clock the roof was covered in a sheet of ice, the driveway was impassable, and the house was plunged into darkness when the power went out. It was clear that the party was not going to happen, and there was no way Virginia and I were going to make it home either.

It was already getting dark, so Virginia gathered up candles and flashlights while I lit the woodstove.

"Kate?" Beth's voice came weakly from the bedroom.

I pushed open the door. "Hey, love! What's up?"

"Can you help me to the bathroom? I'm not feeling too well."

Beth slowly swung her feet over the side of the bed and stood up. When she did, she doubled over, grabbed her belly, and gasped. Then she looked up at me in horror. "My water just broke!"

This is not happening, I thought to myself. *This is not happening.*

"Oh God," she moaned. "Please," she said, reaching for my hand, "help me to the bathroom—I really need to poop!"

I couldn't help but chuckle, and that wore off the initial shock and, blessedly, allowed years of training to kick in. "I've got a better idea, Beth. You need to lie back down and let me check you."

"I can't! I can't be in labor, Kate, I can't! Dilly's not even here!"

"Easy, girl," I said as jovially as I could. "This baby may be just like you and have her own ideas."

I leaned out into the hallway. "Virginia! Can you come here, please?"

Virginia's head popped around the door. "Oh shit!" she said when she saw me sitting between Beth's legs.

I looked up. "Beth's in labor and her water broke. Can you make it to the car and grab my jump kit?"

Dilly, as paramedic captain for Highton Fire and Rescue, insisted that those of us who carried pagers and often had to respond from our homes keep quick-response trauma kits and oxygen in our cars at all times. The kits had proven useful on many occasions when we happened upon accidents or arrived at a call before the aid rig did.

While Virginia headed to the car, I checked Beth. First I gently but firmly palpated the baby's position, or lie. By this time in a normal pregnancy the baby's head should have been low. I pushed again, feeling for the head, but couldn't locate it.

"Beth," I asked her, keeping my voice as nonchalant as I could, "is there any chance your baby could be breech?"

Beth gasped. "I don't know! The doctor told me at my last visit she hadn't turned yet." Tears filled her eyes. "Oh my God, Kate, what are we going to do? Can you call Dilly? Can you get him here?"

Beth was panicking, and I took her hands in mine. I said slowly and firmly, "You and this baby are going to be all right. I'll call Dilly and tell him to get his ass home now and bring the rig as well. Don't you worry; we'll see that you have this baby safe and snug in the hospital."

"But the roads, the ice—" she wailed.

"Let us worry about that. You just worry about relaxing and taking care of this little baby, okay?" I smiled at her.

Beth grinned weakly at me. "Okay."

Virginia showed up with the kit, and I donned some gloves, pulled out the OB gear, the Doppler, stethoscope, and BP cuff. Beth's blood pressure and vitals were normal; the baby's heartbeat was 160 and steady. When Beth's water broke it was clear—there was no evidence of meconium staining, an indicator of fetal distress. I jelled up the Doppler and placed it on Beth's belly. The soft swooshing of the placenta and the rapid thumps of the baby's heartbeat filled the room.

"See?" I told Beth. "She sounds perfect."

We already knew the baby would be a girl, and Dilly and Beth had chosen the name Rae Ann for her.

"Come on, Rae Ann," I said with a smile, "your momma and poppa are waiting for you."

Virginia was standing beside the bed, open-mouthed. "I've never heard a baby's heartbeat before."

"It's beautiful, isn't it?" Beth said softly.

I went into the kitchen under the guise of getting some water, picked up the phone, and dialed 911. Ellen, the dispatcher, answered.

"Police, fire, medical. What are you reporting?"

"Ellen, it's Kate Jacobs."

"Kate! Oh thank goodness! We've been paging you for almost an hour. We need you at the station, if you can get here. The west-end grocery store is on fire, and the ice has wrecks stacked up front to back. We're so short-handed we can't—"

"Ellen," I interrupted. "I'm not calling in response to your page. I've got an emergency too. I'm at Dilly and Beth's. Beth is in labor, her water has broken—and it's breech."

"Oh crap." For a moment the usually calm Ellen was speechless.

I read Beth's and the baby's vitals out to Ellen and then waited for her response.

"Hang on, I'm piping you through to Dilly."

Dilly's voice came on the line almost immediately. Behind him I could hear the fire transmissions. It sounded bad.

"Kate, it's Dill! Can you get Beth into the car and head for St. Joseph's?"

"No. The driveway, the roads—they're a sheet of ice. When Virginia went out to get the gear, she fell twice. She said it's impossible."

There was a brief silence on the line.

"Then stay put. I'm heading your way. Get Beth—" There was a crackle and the line went dead.

"Dilly? Ellen? Ellen?" I hung up and tried again. There was no dial tone. Shit! Weren't phone lines supposed to hold up even if the power went out?

I made my way back to the bedroom armed with towels. "I called Dilly," I said cheerfully. "He's on his way."

"Oh thank God," Beth groaned. "Thank God."

I checked her again. "Beth," I said as calmly as I could, "I'd like to try and turn Rae Ann. It may work; it may not. Can we try?"

Beth eyed me for a moment and then nodded. With Virginia's help we placed her in the knee-chest position: on her hands and knees, with her buttocks up. I had Virginia support Beth while I positioned my hands and carefully palpated Rae Ann's position, then slowly and deliberately attempted to move her. Beth groaned.

After several attempts I gave up.

"What now?" Beth asked shakily.

"Nothing." I smiled as reassuringly as I could. "You're just going to have to deliver a bald-headed baby."

"Wh-what?"

I grinned. "Butt first. Leave it to Dilly and Beth's kid to come into the world back-asswards."

Beth managed a weak laugh. I smiled. Good. At least she was no longer panicked.

A good two hours went by before we heard the sound of a vehicle slithering up the drive. It skidded to a stop, and Dilly burst into the room. He was wet and dirty, still wearing his bunker gear, and he smelled of smoke. I thought he was the most beautiful thing I had ever seen.

He crossed the room in two strides and went down on his knees beside his wife.

"I'm here, baby," he said, pulling her into his arms. "I'm here."

Dilly was all business now. After comforting Beth, he shifted into medic mode. Dillon Bracks was a good medic, a damned good medic. I had learned that quickly in the first few months we had been working together. He had originally hoped to go to medical school, but as the oldest son in a mountain family of six kids, it wasn't going to happen. He made it through the new medic program instead, graduating at the top of his class. When I asked him why he had chosen to come back to Highton County when he could easily have taken a job in any major U.S. city, Dilly had smiled.

"I'm a mountain man, Kate. I was born here, grew up here, and I'll probably die here. Everybody with an EMT-P is going to want to go where the action is—the gunshots, the drugs, the huge fires, the big wrecks, the big cities. Who wants to take on what we do? The farm accidents, elderly patients and all their maladies..."

"The head-on collisions, barn fires, climbing accidents, swift-water rescues," I interjected, teasing him. Highton County wasn't the big city, but it sure wasn't boring.

Dilly loved what he did, and he did it well. Now he checked Beth carefully.

"Is there time to get her to the hospital?" I asked. "After all, you got here."

"That's because I drove the disaster rig," he said. "And just barely." The disaster rig could not transport patients and was only used as a backup to carry gear into remote areas. It had huge, knobby tires and carried a ton of gear, but that was all it was good for. It had a top speed of thirty mph and always reminded me of a miniaturized tank.

"I almost didn't make it," Dilly confessed. "The roads are horrible. And," he said, smiling at his wife, "this little girl is trying hard to make her debut. I'd rather deliver her here than in a ditch somewhere."

Dilly looked up at Virginia and me. "Virginia, can you stoke the fire? And then hang as many big, fluffy towels around it as you can, to warm them up? Kate, can you set up the surg set, the IV kit, and the meds?"

"Surg set? Why?" Beth had been gasping through a contraction and now she struggled to sit up.

"No reason, just the usual precautions I take. Rae Ann's doing great. But I want everything out and in place in case she needs a bit of help."

"She's okay, Dilly, really? She's okay, right?"

"Shh," he soothed her, "you're both doing super. If you need to worry, I'll tell you."

I set up a sterile field and placed the sterile instruments on it, out of Beth's sight. Scalpel, retractors, clamps, forceps, scissors, suture material...I pulled out the meds and sterile gloves for Dilly, drew up morphine, epinephrine, and lidocaine. I placed the bulb syringe and delivery kit at Dilly's side, then set up the IV kit.

I took Beth's vitals and re-checked Rae Ann's heart tones. Everything looked good—except this baby was coming out backward. A field delivery was risky, a field breech even worse. The safest place for this mother and her baby was an OB operating suite, but that was not going to happen this time. Dilly remained calm, alternating his professionalism with tenderness and even kibitzing with his wife. I thought about my very first delivery of Angelina's baby, Tyrone, from what seemed a lifetime ago. I was scared then; I was even more scared now.

"Bethie, I'm going to start an IV, and Kate is going to put a little bit of oxygen on you."

Beth gave the expected cry of alarm. "Why? What's wrong?"

"Nothing," Dilly assured her. "It's standard for an out-of-hospital delivery, and the oh-two will give Rae Ann just a smidge more energy."

Dilly slipped the IV catheter into his wife's hand while I filled the non-rebreather and adjusted it on her face.

"Sing something," Dillon said to Virginia and me. "And don't tell me no, Kate Jacobs, because rumor around this town is you can sing."

I groaned. Sing? Now?

"Sing!" Dillon ordered.

"What?"

"Know any Beatles?" Beth asked from behind her mask.

"Beatles?" I took a deep breath and began to sing: "Can't buy me love, everybody tells me so..." I broke off and glared at Virginia. "Sing, girl!"

She took a deep breath and joined me, "...can't buy me love, no, no, no..."

And so on for maybe three more lines. Then: "Stop singing, oh GOD, stop singing!" Beth screamed.

We fell silent at once, deeply embarrassed. Then I saw that Dilly was applying counterpressure to Beth's perineum, and I slipped to his side to assist. Maybe our singing wasn't the problem.

"Virginia, hold Beth up. Get behind her and let her lean against you." Dilly was all business now.

Beth gave another scream, and a tiny foot poked out of her vagina. A footling presentation. This was going from bad to worse.

Dilly, however, remained completely calm. "You're doing great, sweetheart," he soothed. He reached in with a gloved hand and worked the tiny leg loose.

"Stop it," Beth panted. "Whatever you're doing, stop! It hurts, it hurts!"

"I'm sorry, baby. Bear with me just a bit longer. Rae Ann is almost here."

Dilly worked the second leg loose, and this was followed by an explosive grunt from Beth. The baby's bottom slipped out. Dilly supported his daughter's torso, then reached up and placed his hand in Beth's vagina, supporting the baby's head and clearing a place for her nose. Once the torso delivered, the baby would take a breath. Without an airway, she would suffocate. Dilly's hand provided this.

"Kate, glove up and grab the scalpel."

"Scalpel?" Beth's voice rose to a scream.

"I might need to do an episiotomy, sweetheart. If I don't, you won't like me next time I tell you I want to make love."

"I never want to make love with you ever again!" Beth hollered.

Dilly grinned. "Change of plans, Kate. Take your hand and put it where mine is. Keep the vaginal floor away from the baby's face. She's already breathing."

I slid my hand in beside his, and he pulled his out. He grabbed the scissors and carefully made a small cut. Beth gave another scream, and Rae Ann Bracks slid into her father's waiting hands.

At five a.m. the rain began, melting away the ice and leaving the roads clear. The ambulance made it through, and Virginia and I helped load an exhausted but happy Beth into the rig, Rae Ann bundled in warm towels in her mother's arms.

Dilly stopped before climbing into the rig behind them. He turned to Virginia and me.

"Thanks," he said simply. But his eyes said it all.

The First Rule of EMS:
Never Become a Victim Yourself

The weather had turned bitterly cold, bringing with it a temporary lull in intakes. I was able to close out a number of cases and finish up court reports. Judge Dawley seemed to be a bit less beastly during this time, and I attributed it to bringing fewer cases before him. Nonetheless, I still hated the man and had never forgotten how he had treated his son.

One of the ways I survived the emotional turmoil of my job was to jog. Even on the hottest or coldest days of the year, I would lace on my running shoes at lunch and take off. I would start on the high school track, then wind my way to the county park and along the creek that meandered through the center of town and into the lake. On the days I couldn't run at lunch, I ran in the forest behind our little farm, which was located in an isolated area of Highton County on what had once been a large cattle spread.

Over the years the land had been parceled off and sold, and our small farmhouse, the original ranch house built in the 1920s, sat on the rear of the old estate. It boasted seven pastured acres. The land backed against a one-hundred-acre tract of state forestland, in the center of which was a small lake. A waterfall cascaded from a bluff into the lake, and on summer days I would often jog the rugged trail to the top of the bluff, then jump into the water. It was heavenly!

During our second winter on the farm, Peter and I discovered that the falls froze over. None of my friends had ever done any ice climbing before, and we may not have discovered this amazing sport but for the arrival of another couple, Donna and Neil Preston, to Highton County.

Neil was a former computer programmer and had been working for Hewlett Packard somewhere in Tennessee when he decided to leave the corporate world behind. Not being city folks, the couple headed into the mountains to see if they could find a more "off the beaten path" place to live. They landed in Highton not far from our farm.

Both Donna and Neil happened to be EMTs too, and Dilly and I were introduced to them during an EMT recertification class. Like us, Donna and Neil loved bicycling, hiking, rock climbing, skiing—and ice climbing. The two of them taught the rest of us how to climb the frozen waterfall using ice axes and crampons. In turn we taught them how to run white-water rivers.

A firm friendship developed, and after the birth of Rae Ann, Dilly, Beth, Virginia, and I grew closer than ever. I found myself completely content living in Highton with these wonderful friends. I knew I wouldn't be staying here forever, though—raising kids in rural Appalachia was not what I or Peter wanted to do. We knew our time in Highton would most likely end in a few years. But for now I had a job I loved, Peter was making a fairly decent salary, and we had a wonderful circle of close friends. Plus, the two of us had gone into counseling to try and heal our crumbling marriage.

Not too long ago, the counselor had urged us to set one day a week aside for ourselves, and we chose Thursday nights as our "date night." The rule was that on this night we were to do something together and not let work or anything else interfere.

This particular Thursday was supposed to be date night, but it was also Virginia's birthday. Peter and I agreed that we would spend it having an informal dinner for her at our place. Hilary had scheduled an all-staff meeting that morning that was to have lasted all day, but we finished early and I found myself not in the least bit interested in working at my desk for the rest of the day. Since the entire "Chaos Troop" was coming over for Virginia's birthday dinner, I wanted to get home and start cooking.

Virginia had requested Hungarian beef stew, one of my specialties. I begged off from work, and Hilary waved me out the door. It was still early, and despite a newly fallen powder-sugar dusting of snow, I was itching for a run. I put the pot of beef stew on the stove to simmer on low, laced on my sneakers, pulled a warm fleece jacket over my running clothes, donned a hat and mittens, and took off for the waterfall.

The trail was icy, and I ran more slowly than usual. As a result, it took a good bit longer to reach the falls. Daylight would soon start fading, and I knew it was best not to linger. Still, I had promised Dilly earlier that I would check out the waterfall to see if it was frozen enough for climbing. Carefully I made my way up the trail and to the top of the falls. It was a bit precarious standing up there, especially in nothing but running shoes, so I stayed back from the edge as I surveyed the ice, which I saw was still too thin and brittle to climb.

As I turned to head back down, I heard a crack and then a whistling behind me. Without warning a huge tree limb smacked me in the back, knocking me forward. I lost my footing and scrambled to regain my balance, but to no avail. My feet shot out from under me and I felt myself sliding and then hurtling the almost twenty feet to the fall's base. The last thing I remember was screaming.

When I came to, it was dark, and I had no idea where I was. I was cold, terribly cold, and I was shivering violently. My head ached horribly, I smelled vomit, and I tasted blood. I groaned. I lay still for a moment, trying desperately to get my bearings. Then memory flooded back. I was lying at the base of the waterfall. I vaguely remembered that a branch had smacked me in the back. It must have cracked off one of the large hickories that grew alongside the fall and knocked me down. I sat up slowly, which made my head spin.

I waited a few moments and then gingerly tried to stand. A searing pain shot through my right ankle, and I collapsed into the snow. There was just enough moonlight coming through the trees for me to see that my ankle was swollen and misshapen. I'd obviously fractured it. Shit, shit, SHIT! What now?

I buried my face in my hands and waited for the spinning to stop and the nausea to settle. My teeth were chattering, and I knew that if I didn't get out of there, I could die of hypothermia. I grabbed a large stick and, using it as a crutch, once again attempted to stand. Once again pain, nausea, and dizziness forced me back down.

There was no help for it. I was stuck here. I had broken the cardinal rule of the out-of-doors: I had come out into the woods completely unprepared, wearing nothing but my running clothes, a fleece jacket, hat, and mittens. I had no flashlight, no whistle, nothing.

I started to cry. And then I got mad, really mad. There was no way I was going to sit here and succumb to hypothermia. I gritted my teeth, grabbed the stick again, and forced myself to stand. Then slowly, painfully, I began to hobble down the trail. I was almost to the road when I heard voices calling my name.

"I'm here!" I screamed. "Help!"

It was Donna who reached me first, followed by Neil and the others. Dilly wanted to call for the rig, but I refused. They splinted my leg, stuffed me in the car, and we headed for the hospital. An x-ray confirmed the ankle was broken, and I was kept overnight for observation.

It took almost three months for the ankle to heal. In the meantime I hobbled around the farm and the office on crutches, with a backpack to hold my briefs and files. The neighbors were incredibly gracious in helping with errands and chores; I hadn't realized how many friends Peter and I had made.

Virginia and I swapped cars, since hers was an automatic and mine a clutch and it was impossible to drive a stick with a cast on my leg. One evening Virginia called me, upset, to tell me that while she had been at work, somebody had keyed my car and destroyed the paint on the passenger side. We checked with our insurance company, but the repair would be less than the deductible, so I spent several days sanding and painting the damage. It didn't look that great, but it was somewhat better, so I considered myself satisfied. I had other things, like a broken ankle and a heavy caseload, to worry about.

Late Night Gatherings

My pager went off one night as I was leaving work, and I was called out to place a child. The only available foster parent was hours away in the direction of Asheville, and so it was after midnight before I turned up the road that led to our farm.

Peter was gone on a business trip, and I knew the house would be dark and cold. Very few cars came down our road since it simply circled back on itself, and only two other families lived on the former cattle farm with us. We truly had the neighborhood practically to ourselves.

The farm was always peaceful and quiet, and I had never been afraid of being home alone. In fact, it wasn't uncommon for me to pull my mattress onto the screened back porch and sleep out there on summer nights, listening to the crickets and the call of the whippoorwills. Even in the summer it was cooler on the farm than in the town of Highton, and it was rare that Peter or I turned on our little window-unit air conditioner.

Peter and I had adopted a stray cat; or rather, he had adopted us, by wandering into our kitchen one summer evening and refusing to leave. The fact that I had fed him sardines probably didn't help, but the cat became ours—or we became his—and he always acted as the enthusiastic welcoming committee whenever Peter or I got home from work.

The cat, a big, friendly tabby named Bjorn after a character in a J.R.R. Tolkien book, had one very bad habit, however. Peter had installed a fifty-gallon fish tank in our living room, and Bjorn loved to sit on top of it, pry open the lid, and attempt to fish out some dinner.

We tried everything to keep him out: put weights on it, taped it down, and even tied it with wire, but to no avail. Bjorn managed to get it loose, and thus we occasionally found the head of an unlucky angelfish or other cichlid lying on our pillow as a gift from a proud Bjorn.

As I turned up the dark road to our farm that night, I wondered what type of mischief Bjorn had gotten into this time. He usually dreamed up some sort of revenge if we were late feeding him, and it was certainly well past his suppertime by now. Had he emptied the aquarium of fish once again or maybe decided to use one of Peter's best shoes for a litter box?

My musings were cut short by a rather surprising sight: As I was turning around a tight bend in the road, my headlights briefly illuminated a group of men, perhaps a half dozen of them, standing in the field not far from our house. When the headlights caught them, they turned slowly and stared at my car, then, as one, they all sank down into the tall grass.

A chill went through me, and I drove hurriedly up to the house and quickly let myself into the kitchen. I locked the door behind me and drew the blinds. Who were those men and what were they doing in the field at this hour? And why had they ducked down as if they were trying to avoid my headlights?

Nobody hunted out here at night, and nothing was in season anyway. So what were they up to? And who the heck were they?

In spite of the late hour, I called Beth and Dilly. A sleepy Beth answered, but she snapped awake when I told her what I had seen.

"Dilly's at the station tonight," she said at once. "I'll have him call you, okay?"

"Yes, please, Beth."

She must have heard the shakiness of my voice, because she asked gently, "Want me and Rae Ann to come and stay with you? Or do you want to come here?"

By then I'd decided that Peter's absence and the lateness of the hour had made my imagination go into overdrive. I told her thanks, but it was probably some hunters or something, and that I'd wait for Dilly's call.

Dilly phoned me back shortly, and I repeated to him what I'd seen, including the strange behavior the men had shown when my headlights had strobed them.

Dilly didn't seem at all surprised. "It's probably the survivalists."

"The what?" I asked.

"Survivalists. Hasn't anyone told you about them?"

"No."

"They own a compound a few hours from here. Rumor has it it's stocked with guns and ammo. They're wacko but harmless. They just like to drive out to different places in the county, stalk neighborhoods, and see if they can get through people's backyards without being detected."

"Pretty creepy, if you ask me."

Dilly laughed. "Yeah. They're all kind of strange, but they haven't hurt anybody yet. Still, you want to go spend the night with Beth and Rae?"

"Do you think I need to?"

"Nah," Dilly assured me. "Like I said, they've been around for a while. And they really are harmless, unless you're a commie pinko or, worse, not white."

"Dilly!" I was shocked. "I thought I left that sort of disgusting talk behind in South Carolina!"

"Easy, girl. I'm just quoting them. They're bigots for sure, but they wouldn't harm an all-American green-eyed redhead like you. In fact, they probably see their life mission as protecting poor, defenseless women like you and Beth."

"Oh peachy," I snorted. "My heroes!"

"Well, if it makes you feel better, keep your doors locked, but I'm pretty sure you're fine."

Dilly's words comforted me some, but I still slept uneasily.

The next morning there was no sign of any gathering in the field, and I wondered if I had just imagined anyone being out there at all.

"Life is What Happens to Us While We Are Busy Making Other Plans"
(John Lennon)

Summer had arrived, and it was hot and sweltering, even in the mountains where we lived. Peter and I were still in counseling, but we didn't seem to be making any progress. We hadn't made love in a long time, but I kept hoping things might improve. We held to our Thursday date nights, and these were usually fun, so we kept at them. At least we didn't fight. But nowadays it was the silent indifference that bothered me the most.

Peter had gone back to school to pursue a PhD. It meant more time spent in the distant city at the "U," but we felt it was worth it. On this particular Thursday, Peter told me that he would have to exchange our date night for another one. Seems he had a paper due and wanted to spend the evening finishing it at the university library. I told him sure, but inwardly I was disappointed.

When I got home from work and stepped into the silent house, I suddenly decided that I didn't want to spend the evening alone and that I would drive to the university and surprise Peter, take him out for some fancy city food, and then let him finish working. I made reservations for two at a nice restaurant, dressed up in a sexy skirt, blouse, and heels, smeared some makeup on my face, dabbed on perfume, and hit the road.

When I reached the outskirts of the city, my car was running on fumes, so

I pulled into the gas station to fill up before heading to the university. The station was at the biggest intersection of the main road into town, and I turned to watch the traffic roll by as the tank filled.

The light turned red, and to my surprise I saw Peter's car pull up to the intersection not ten feet from me and stop. The window was open and music drifted out—music and a woman's laughter. My hand dropped from the pump, and I peered closer. Sure enough, there was Peter sitting with a striking blonde in the front seat, his arm around her, her head resting on his chest. The light changed, and Peter glanced in my direction. I swear he saw me, but he turned away and headed down the road. I saw the car turn into El Toreador, a Mexican restaurant where we sometimes ate on date night.

I hung up the pump and stumbled blindly to my car. There had to be an explanation! Peter couldn't be, he wouldn't be cheating on me, would he? She must be a co-worker or a fellow student…but I knew I was deluding myself.

I drove slowly down the street and turned into the lot just past El Toreador. Feeling like a heel, I walked around the back of the restaurant and sidled up to a window. It was getting dark, and I doubted anyone would see me. It took a moment, but I spotted Peter and the woman. They were sitting at a table, two margaritas in front of them, holding hands. Tears welled in my eyes. Part of me wanted to march inside and demand an explanation; the other part wanted to crawl under a bush and die.

I turned and stumbled back to my car. I sat there for a long time, debating on what to do. Finally I started the engine and headed back to the highway. Driving almost blindly, I ended up in the driveway of Stephan and Virginia's house. They were watching TV when I knocked, and Virginia welcomed me with a huge smile.

"Hey, Kate! How's the ankle?"

"Fine," I said, "it's healed fine."

She took a look at my face. "Kate, are you okay?"

Tears welled again, and I shook my head no. She led me to the sofa, and Stephan turned off the TV.

"I just saw Peter with another woman," I managed to choke out.

Virginia and Stephan exchanged looks over my head, and a sudden, sick realization washed over me. "You know?" I asked incredulously. "You know?"

Virginia sighed and tried to cover my hand with hers, but I shook it off. "We didn't know how to tell you, hon. He's been seeing her for a few weeks."

I stared at them, aghast. "You knew and you didn't tell me?" I leaped to my feet, hurt—hurt, embarrassed, and angry. "I thought you were my friends! How could you betray me like this?"

"Kate," Stephan said quietly, "your marriage has been over for a long time."

I wheeled on him. "So it's okay for him to commit adultery?"

"I didn't say that."

"Jesus, Stephan, why didn't you tell me?" I sat back down and buried my face in my hands as hot tears washed down my cheeks. "Who else knows?" I whispered.

Virginia looked guilty. "We all do—except Neil and Donna. I don't think they know."

For a moment I sat there unable to talk. "How did you find out?" I finally asked, almost afraid to hear the answer.

Virginia looked at Stephan again, and I saw the color rise to her face.

"The truth, please," I begged.

Virginia sighed heavily. "Peter brought her to a party at Dilly and Beth's a while back. The last time you were up north visiting your family..." Her voice trailed off.

"So Dill and Beth are in on this too."

"If it's any comfort, Beth told them to leave."

I closed my eyes as the room spun around me. "Thanks," I said, standing up and heading for the door. "Thanks for nothing."

It was bad enough that Peter had betrayed me, but the betrayal of my friends hurt even worse.

It was well after midnight before Pete came home. I heard the door close softly and the kitchen light go on. I got up to find Peter sitting at the table.

I sat down beside him. "Why?" I asked.

"Kate, I'm sorry..."

"I don't want to hear it. I want to know why."

"I don't know," he said without looking at me. "It just...happened."

"I trusted you! We took vows…"

"Our marriage has been over for a long time," he said, echoing Stephan's words. "You're never here anymore. You're married to your work. You're not the same woman I married."

There was truth in what he was saying, and I nodded.

"I'm sorry," Peter said again. "I'll make this as easy on you as I can." He got up and began to pull some of his clothing out of the dresser.

"Pete," I said, "wait, please. We can make this work."

He turned fully to face me. "No, we can't."

He got in the car and drove out of my life.

I picked up Bjorn and sat on the porch swing with him on my lap, but for some odd reason I couldn't cry.

I called in sick the next day but went back to work on Monday. I put on a happy face, but I could tell that Hilary sensed something was wrong. Rather than give her the chance to confront me, I grabbed an intake from the basket and headed for the high school, where a sixteen-year-old had told her guidance counselor that her stepfather had raped her.

I arrived at the guidance counselor's office the same time Bob Morris did. I plastered on what I hoped was my usual cheerful face and went in to interview the teen. I did all the usual things a good counselor does: I leaned forward, nodded, and paraphrased back some of the things she said. I encouraged her and empathized and reassured her that I was there to help. But as she spoke, a little voice in my head whispered, *Why don't you tell somebody who gives a damn? Because I don't anymore.*

It wasn't just the emptiness of Peter's and our friends' betrayal. I was burned out, and I knew it. Too many years in the field; years of listening to horror stories and trying to put the pieces of children's shattered lives back together. I knew suddenly I was done.

I arranged for the teen to stay with an aunt, filed the paperwork, and left a message for her mother. Then I returned to the office and knocked on Hilary's door.

"Hey, Hil," I said when she invited me inside. She motioned to the usual chair by the window, and I sat down.

"I'm giving my notice, Hilary," I said softly.

She sighed and nodded. "I'm not surprised, Kate. You've been at this a long, long time." She studied my face for a moment. "How soon before you want to wrap it up?"

"Two weeks?" I asked.

Hilary stood up and pushed her door shut. "I haven't told the unit yet, but there's a hiring freeze on. If someone quits, we can't replace them. If you go, we're down a worker despite our intakes being up."

"Oh God, Hilary," I groaned, "please don't guilt trip me."

"I'm sorry," she said, turning to face me. "I don't mean to. I'm just trying to make this as painless on the others as I can."

I thought for a moment. "How about if I stay until the end of the summer? I can start closing out cases as fast as possible, and if you cut back—or preferably eliminate my intakes—then it won't be such a jolt for the others."

There was a knock, and Deanne poked her head around the door. "I'm sorry to interrupt. Kate, your brother is on the phone long distance from Connecticut. He says it's important."

I closed my office door and lifted the receiver. "Hey, bro."

"Hey, sis." Kurt's voice was gentle, and I knew immediately something was wrong. "What's going on?"

"It's Dad, Kate. He's had a stroke. Mom wants you to come."

I closed my eyes. What else? What else could possibly go wrong? I'd just lost my husband to another woman, been betrayed by my closest friends, quit my job...and now my beloved dad had had a stroke.

"How bad?"

"We won't know until morning."

I buried my face in my hands.

"Kate? You still there?"

"Yeah," I said. "I'm still here. I'll see what flight I can catch. I'll call you right back."

When God Closes a Door, Somewhere He Opens a Window

The cardiac monitor beeped softly, and I settled back in the chair and closed my eyes. I was exhausted; mentally, physically, and spiritually exhausted. I had railed at God on the flight to Connecticut, but it seemed God was watching out for me, because when Kurt met me at the airport, he was able to tell me that our father was out of the woods.

"He won't ever be quite the same, but he's going to make it."

I spent three long days in the hospital with my father, reviewing his care plan with the staff, arranging for his rehabilitation, and just sitting by him, holding his hand or talking to him whenever my mother or other siblings weren't able to be there. Every day he grew stronger, spoke more clearly, and regained some of the motor function the stroke had taken from him.

The neurologist was delighted with his progress and felt that while he would not make a full recovery, his prognosis was excellent. By the fourth day my mother and I felt comfortable enough to leave the hospital and make plans for some family time for all of us.

That night we sat around the dining room table gorging ourselves. Mom had decided that the best way to celebrate my father's prognosis was to cook an enormous meal for us. And so we feasted on roast beef, new potatoes, baby peas, and apple crumble for dessert.

I had decided that I was not going to share the news about Pete's and my separation with my family during this visit; the concerns over Dad were causing enough worry without heaping Peter's and my problems on top of them.

The phone rang, and my sister Penny went to answer it. "Kate? It's Peter!" she sang out innocently as she handed me the phone.

"I'll take it in the bedroom, if you don't mind."

"Oh, yeah!" Penny grinned. "Time for that sexy bedroom talk."

I snatched the phone, sat down on the bed, and put the receiver to my ear. "Peter, why are you calling me here?" I asked somewhat curtly.

"Hey, Kate," he said softly in that sexy voice of his. "I heard. I'm sorry about your dad."

"Yeah well, thanks, but he's going to be fine. I don't need your sympathy," I said coldly.

I heard him sigh. "Kate, I'm actually calling you for another reason…" His voice trailed off and he seemed to be groping for the right words.

"What is it?" I asked, wondering what else he could possibly say that would hurt me as much as his betrayal had.

"I'm sorry, I'm so sorry."

I was about to roll my eyes and tell him that he should spare me more apologies when he blurted out in a choked voice, "Our house just burned down."

Stunned silence.

"Wh-what?" I asked stupidly. "What do you mean, 'our house just burned down'?"

"Our house—your house. It's gone. Completely gone."

My mind could not wrap itself around this. "I-I don't understand."

"I just got back from the farm. It was still burning. There was nothing the fire department could do. The fire was so hot…Kate, there's nothing left."

"No!" I said. "I don't believe you!"

"I'm sorry," he said again.

I felt as if I was falling down a pitch-black hole. "How? How did it happen? How did it start? Oh my God! Bjorn! The fish! Did anyone get hurt?"

"Bjorn is fine. Donna found him in the bushes. She and Neil took him to their house. The fish are gone."

It was too much, too much. I sank down on the bed and began to sob.

The door opened, and my mother appeared, looking at me worriedly. "My house burned down!" I cried. And I ran into her arms.

My family finally convinced me that my father was doing so well that there was no reason for me to stay. The neurologist was having him transferred to a rehabilitation unit, and he would be spending another two weeks there. Mom had plenty of help, so there really was nothing I could do. They suggested I go home immediately and take care of things there.

Seeing how distraught I was, Kurt offered to go with me. I argued that Dad and Mom needed him here, but he and Mom were adamant. So were Penny and my other brothers, who assured me they'd stay in Connecticut as long as they needed to.

Kurt and I flew to North Carolina the next morning. On the flight I fessed up to Kurt about Pete's and my marriage and the fact that I had given notice at work.

"Good Lord, Kate." That was all he could say. "Good Lord."

Peter met us at the airport and drove us out to the farm—or rather, what was left of the farm. During the long trip from the airport he talked about nothing but the fire, obviously trying to soften the blow by describing in grim detail what to expect. He said the cause was still under investigation but that the fire marshal had already visited the site.

When we stopped to take a roadside break, Peter opened the trunk and took out a small cardboard box, which smelled somewhat smoky, and handed it to me. I pulled it open and gave a cry of surprise.

When Peter had first phoned me with the news that my house was completely gone, three things had come immediately to mind after the initial shock wore off. The first was concern over Bjorn, the next was the realization that my silly sweetgrass basket was gone, and the third was the loss of the last Christmas letter my grandfather had written to me. My German "Opa" had been a wonderful artist, and every Christmas and birthday he sent each of his grandchildren a lovely, hand-drawn card.

Two Christmases ago he had sent me an exquisite pen-and-ink sketch of a snow-covered pine bough with a lit candle on it and a New England church with a simple steeple, covered in snow.

Opa had died suddenly a few months after I received the card, and I cherished it almost more than anything else I owned. I had always planned to have it professionally framed, but with the pressures of work and everything else, I hadn't gotten around to it. Since then it had been sitting in the single drawer of the small desk I used in the study.

When I opened the box, I found a few items from that desk drawer, including Opa's card. The drawing was a bit charred in one corner but was otherwise unharmed. It was almost as if God had asked me what one thing I would have wanted to save from the house. Peter and I didn't have much in those days, and that card would have been my first choice.

"How did you get this, Peter?" I asked, stunned.

"I didn't. One of your firefighter friends saved it. When they got there, the back of the house was in flames, but the front wasn't burning yet. He busted out the bedroom window and pulled the drawer out thinking maybe there was something in it you needed."

I stared at the singed edge of the card. Here was proof that, even in the darkest hours, God often gave us a single ray of hope to pull us through.

In spite of this and Peter's warning, however, nothing prepared me for the devastation that greeted us when we turned down the road and the farm—my home for the past decade—came into view. Where the house had once stood was a pile of still-smoldering ash and rubble. All that remained was the bottom half of the chimney; the upper portion had collapsed into the debris. That and the brick front porch steps, standing eerily upright and leading to nowhere.

Everything else was gone. The huge walnut tree that had towered majestically over the house had been scorched. Every leaf and many of its branches were missing. One apple tree had fallen over and burned, and my garden was a pool of mud and tire-tracks from the fire trucks.

I got out of the car and stared, disbelieving, dumbstruck, and saddened beyond belief. The rubble was too hot to approach, so Peter drove Kurt and me to Neil and Donna's, who had graciously offered to let us stay with them until I figured out what to do.

The next morning the four of us rose early, put on heavy denim clothing, boots, and gloves, and headed back to the farm. As we pulled up the long drive, I was surprised to see a collection of cars already parked near the rubble.

As Kurt and I got out, Stephan, Virginia, Dilly and Beth, Hilary, and many of my co-workers came up to greet us. Their hugs and support meant everything in the world at that moment.

Stephan folded me in his arms and then pulled back and said, "Sorry, Kate. We wanted to surprise you with a barbeque, but it kinda got out of hand..."

Leave it to Stephan to make me laugh even at the worst of times.

Kurt had called the insurance adjuster from the airport before we left Connecticut, and the agent, a no-nonsense man named Edward Johnson, had told him that the investigation of the fire scene had been completed the day before and to go ahead and sift through the rubble if we wished.

The day was already hot and sweltering, and the sun beat down on the ankle-deep ashes. It was clear that absolutely nothing had survived the inferno. Dilly told me that the house, which had been built in 1920, had been insulated with plaster, mud, and burlap. This insulation trapped the heat in the walls and made it one of the hottest fires the department had ever put out.

"We actually got it out when the structure was still standing, but then it flared up again," he told me. "After that there was nothing left."

I picked my way slowly through the ashes of what, only days before, had been my home. My friends searched through the still-smoldering rubble with me, panting because of the heat and the lingering smoke, trying to find any surviving remnant of my past. Memorabilia, knickknacks, photographs, climbing ropes, mountain rescue gear, a collection of geodes—even a kayak— had all turned to dust along with my clothing and furniture in what Dilly had described as the hottest fire in over a decade.

A silver gleam caught my eye, and I pushed aside the hot ashes with my boot to reveal the ring of what remained of my Canon Rebel S camera. I'd rarely gone anywhere without it, and my family and friends could attest to my passion for photography. The loss of the camera didn't bother me so much; it could be replaced. But what had burned along with my camera were the hundreds of photos I had taken of the foster kids at picnics and Christmas parties, rescue missions I had been on, photos of my family and friends...memories that could never be replaced.

"Kate, look at this! I found one of your geodes!"

Donna's voice was ecstatic as she lifted the beautiful purple crystal out of the rubble. The geodes had been a gift to me from one of my foster kids who wanted to be a geologist when he grew up. I cherished these lovely stones not only for their beauty, but also because of what they represented in this boy: the desire to move beyond the poverty and ignorance into which he had been born and the determination to succeed and be someone special.

When Donna opened her gloved hand and the geode was exposed to the ninety-degree heat of the day, the crystal, still super-heated from the blaze, exploded into a pile of dust.

I took the dust and the camera ring, sat down on a boulder, and cried.

Dilly crouched in front of me. I wiped the tears off my face, leaving a smudge of black soot. He handed me a flask of water and said, "Come on. Let's walk down to the falls. We need to talk."

It was blessedly cool by the falls. The normally heavy spring run-off was down to a summer trickle, and I kicked off my boots and dangled my feet in the water.

Dilly sat down on a rock beside me.

"I hate to keep heaping more on your plate, Kate, but you might as well get the whole story."

I stared at him, bewildered. He sighed heavily. "The insurance guy—Johnson? He's having you investigated for arson."

"What?" I leaped to my feet, shocked beyond belief.

Dilly nodded grimly. "The investigation was quick because the signs were unmistakable. Peter was interviewed, and he's not considered a suspect. I asked him to let me be the one to tell you."

I took a few deep breaths then whirled to face him. "I did not burn my own house down, Dilly! I wasn't even here! I don't know what sick, demented pervert did this or for what reason, but why, why would I ever want to destroy my own things? It makes no sense! I was out of town—out of town because my father suffered a fucking stroke!"

"Easy, Kate, easy! This is all pretty much routine. It was arson, we know that without doubt. The blaze started on the floor of the bedroom as evidenced by kerosene residue. My guess is somebody broke in, lit one of your kerosene lanterns, then smashed it on the floor."

I didn't say a word. I just stood there, my face buried in my hands. Dilly pulled me back down on the boulder. "Routine, I promise. Still, I think you should hire an attorney. There's a lot of legal stuff that needs to be handled, and as I said before, I think you have enough on your plate."

I couldn't look at him. "Anything else I need to know?"

"Not at the moment. I think you've had enough dumped on your head."

Of Devils...

I called Patrick to ask him who the best attorney was to handle my situation.

"Me!" he responded cheerfully.

"You're a family court attorney," I reminded him, "not a criminal arson type."

"No, but I do know a good bit about criminal investigations, as you are well aware. And I have a whole office full of experts at my disposal, plus there will be no charge, because we all love you."

I couldn't help but laugh. "That's a convincing argument. Okay," I agreed.

Kurt and I met with Patrick the next morning. I was surprised when Kay Thompson from the prosecutor's office showed up in Patrick's office.

"We know you didn't burn your own house down, Kate, and we want to be sure your insurance company knows it too. We've asked the agent and investigators to meet us here. Anything they want to know, we'd like to hear too."

I nodded.

It turned out to be a long morning. The investigators asked me a whole bunch of questions, much as they had Peter a few days before, and gradually the focus turned from me to other possibilities.

We discussed my clients—were there any who had threatened me, any who seemed bent on revenge?

I shook my head. "Not that I can think of. Most of the uglier cases ended up in permanency planning. I'd say the staff in that unit is at higher risk of something like this than me."

They called Edward Johnson, the insurance agent, in. He was a heavyset man with a red face and a foul temper. He glared at me, and I got the sense that he had already tried me and found me guilty.

The first thing he did was pull out a stack of photos and hand them to me. I picked them up and gasped. It may have been an inanimate object, but it was my home, and I had loved it. Peter and I had spent years fixing it up, painting it, remodeling and decorating it. When you lose your home, especially through an act of violence, you lose your sense of safety. I wanted to crawl into my bed, pull the covers over my head, and cry myself to sleep, but there was no home, no bed, no covers, nothing left.

The photos showed my house engulfed in flames. They were pouring out of the windows, doors, and chimney. The apple tree looked like a gargantuan torch, and the walnut tree was shriveling in the smoke. But worst of all, peeking out from beneath the boxwood hedges, was a terrified Bjorn.

I looked through the photos again, and then I started to cry. I mean really, really cry. Like I'd cried when I took Erin Wheaton away from the only mother she'd ever known. I cried so hard that Patrick had to fetch me a box of tissues and a glass of water. I cried so hard I was hiccoughing.

And all the while Mr. Johnson sat staring at me with disdain.

Patrick told me later he had wanted to punch him.

Afterward, Kurt took me out to lunch and did his best to cheer me up. And later that night, we had dinner with friends. Their laughter and jokes went a long way to erase the fiery images of those photographs from my mind.

I guess Mr. Johnson wrote in his report that I was not the one who had burned down my house, because the matter was quickly dropped. That should have been a relief, but it wasn't, because the details surrounding the insurance claim quickly took an unpleasant place in my life. And Mr. Johnson turned out to be the kind of agent who proceeded to challenge me on every single item I had ever owned.

First he asked me to make a list of everything that was in the house when it went up in flames. Stupidly Peter and I had never thought to photograph the contents of our home and place those photos in a safe deposit box. So I spent hours and hours between working my cases listing everything I could remember.

Imagine for a moment trying to itemize every last spoon, fork, sock, T-shirt, book, tool, towel, box of thumbtacks, photo album, roll of toilet paper, appliances, furniture, draperies, pillows, blankets, sheets…every last item you own. Then list the number, age, weight, size, name brand, and condition of every single one of those items while you're still largely in shock over their loss.

I found the task to be nearly impossible. In fact, for many years after the fire I would ask myself, *Now where did I leave my…?* And then I'd remember, *Oh, yeah, it fried.*

After receiving the list, Mr. Johnson went over it with a fine-toothed comb and questioned *every single* item, as if I had made them all up.

"Climbing ropes? Harnesses?" he sniffed. "You're suggesting then, Mrs. Jacobs, that you're a big rock climber?"

"As a matter of fact," Patrick answered icily (he was, of course, present at this meeting), "Mrs. Jacobs helped start the mountain rescue unit here in Highton. She's one of only two women on the high-angle rescue team."

Kay Thompson, who had also insisted on sitting in with me, nodded emphatically. "Mr. Johnson, I remember going to a party at Kate's house one day and opening the wrong door when I was looking for the bathroom. It was your guestroom, I think, Kate. You had all these ropes, pulleys, harnesses, and other stuff hung up in it. I remember thinking, 'wow, either this lady is really kinky, or she's into climbing.'"

"Climbing," I assured her, smiling back at her bleakly.

In fact, I'd completely lost my sense of humor by then, and it only got worse as the insurance company and I went around and around for days. Kurt and Patrick took on the biggest burdens of argument, and in the end, I was awarded a check for $35,000.

It was a pittance, as it came nowhere near what it would take to replace an entire house and all its furnishings, appliances, dishes, and clothing, not to mention everything else I had lost. It seemed odd to think that everything you own in the world can be summed up in one neat little check.

But the greatest losses were those things—like the photographs and geodes—that could never be replaced. And those had been priceless.

…And Dragons

Life settled back into a routine; an odd routine, but one that allowed me to keep moving while reassessing where to go next. Donna and Neil encouraged me and Bjorn to stay with them for the duration of my stay in Highton, and I continued to work, closing out as many cases as I could, still with the intention of leaving by the first of September.

It was a hot, beautiful Friday evening in late August when Donna knocked on my bedroom door. "Phone for you. He didn't say who it was."

I picked up the receiver. "'Lo?"

"Hey, Kate, it's Bob Morris. How you holdin' up?"

I hadn't talked with the detective since well before the fire. "Hey, Bob," I answered. "It's nice to hear your voice." I sighed. "I'm holding up as well as can be expected. Upright, breathing, putting one foot in front of the other."

"Kate, I'm sorry for your loss. But I'm wondering if you could meet me out at your farm?" he asked.

"Sure. When?"

"How about now?"

"Now? I-I guess so. What's up?"

"Well," Bob said a bit evasively, "let's talk about that when we both get there."

I was sitting on what was left of the front steps when Bob drove up. To my surprise, Reverend Avery Jessup from Nona's church was with him. The sun was just starting to set over the valley, reminding me of how beautiful the farm had been and how acutely I felt its loss.

177

"Hey, Miz Kate," the minister said, folding me in an enormous hug. "I'm so sorry, baby. This should never have happened to you."

"It could have been so much worse, Reverend. At least no one got hurt."

"Well, actually it could have been a lot worse. But that's why we're here." The minister looked angry as he spoke.

I shook Bob's hand, and the three of us settled down on the steps.

"I understand you went through the insurance investigation from hell, beggin' your pardon, Reverend," Bob began.

"Yes, he was such a pleasant chap," I answered sarcastically, knowing he was referring to agent Edward Johnson.

Bob grinned. "You haven't lost your sense of humor at least."

"It's about the only thing I didn't lose."

"Well, you came pretty close to losing a heck of a lot more," Bob said softly. He leaned back against the step and studied my face. "You're not going to like hearing what I have to tell you, and I'm pretty sure it's going to impact what you do next." He hesitated then asked, "Does the name Mertz mean anything to you?"

I thought hard. Mertz, Mertz...I knew that name. Mertz...

"Yes," I answered. "I did an intake on the Mertz family a number of years ago. Pretty ugly case of gross child neglect, physical abuse, sexual assault. It wasn't on my caseload long because it got transferred into permanency planning pretty fast. I do remember the father went to jail for a while."

"And what do you know about the KKK?" Bob asked.

"The Ku Klux Klan?" I frowned. "Very little. Why?"

The reverend and the detective exchanged glances, and then Reverend Jessup sighed heavily. "We strongly suspect they're the ones who burned your house down, baby."

It took a while to find my voice. "What? No way! The KKK? Here in Highton County? Oh, come on!"

"Kate—" Bob tried to interrupt.

"And with all due respect, Reverend, I'm white. I thought they just went after minorities?"

"Or social workers who take their kids away and put one of the Grand

Dragon's right-hand men in jail," Bob said sharply.

I looked at him, stunned. "A Grand Dragon? You mean they—they have leaders and everything? But—but this isn't the Deep South, this is North Carolina!"

"Abel and Jessica Mertz's father is cousin to the Grand Dragon of the KKK here—kind of like a local leader. The Highton County chapter is pretty large," Bob explained. "In fact, you'd be surprised how many of the men you know personally are members."

They waited a few minutes for this to sink in. I reached down and scooped up a pile of ash and let it sift through my fingers.

"Detective Morris and I do undercover work together," the minister finally said. "We've been following the clan for years. When members of my church were victimized the first time, Detective Morris came out to work with us. We've been doing so ever since."

"Go on," I said.

"Do you remember Mertz's son, Abel?"

I thought back to the sullen, overweight twins I'd tried to help so long ago. "Yes. He was very angry that I got involved with his family."

"Well," Bob said, "he was more than angry. When his father was sent to jail, Abel swore he'd avenge him. He blamed you for turning his sister against the family."

I remembered how his sister Jessica's testimony had helped turn the case. "Holy hell," I breathed. "But he was just a kid at the time, and this was years ago."

The minister smiled sadly. "Time don't mean nothing when hatred burns. And the clan likes to give warnings. We suspect Mertz gave his son permission from prison to 'give you a slap.' Except that little 'slap' almost cost you and Miss Virginia your lives."

It took a moment for that to sink in. "My car?" I breathed.

Bob nodded. "We can't verify this, but we suspect Abel Mertz messed with the brake lines on your VW."

"We could have died," I gasped. "And the kids...he almost killed a bus load of innocent kids!"

Bob nodded. "Which is why Abel was chastised at a clan meeting not too long afterward, though again we can't verify that was the reason."

"But that was so long ago," I protested.

"Anger festers," Bob said grimly. "Like his father, Abel spent a lot of years in and out of jail, first JuVee, then prison. Back when he tampered with your brakes and Mertz Senior found out his boy had been chastised for that, he called the rest of the clan a bunch of 'lily-livered pansies.' Far as we can tell, they ostracized him, and Abel too. We don't know where the father's living now, but Abel turned up here not too long ago."

Long enough to key my car when Virginia was driving it? I wondered. Should I have said something to Bob then? But how could I have known?

I swallowed hard. "How do you know all this?"

"We've been working this case a long while," Bob said evasively.

"Around here it's hard to make people talk," Reverend Jessup added.

"We think Abel Mertz, now of legal age, came back to settle old scores," Bob continued. "Apparently there was some debate about burning your house when the Mertz case first went down years ago. But some of the Coward Boys—that's another name we use for the KKK—who live around here know you and how much you've done for the county both as an EMT and with the DSS. They refused to consider it."

"But maybe it gave Abel Mertz the idea, and he couldn't let it go," Reverend Jessup put in. He smiled without humor. "Don't feel so bad, honey. You ain't the only one he's been targeting since he came back."

I sat there stunned, unable to comprehend any of this.

"So," Bob went on, "we think he's been watching you along with some other folks I can't tell you about, and he and his pals, also former members of the Coward Boys, knew exactly when you went out of town."

I felt ill. "I think I saw them one night. I drove home late and there was a bunch of creepy-looking guys in the field by the house. I was so scared, I called Dilly. He said they were survivalists..." My voice trailed off. "Dilly? Please tell me Dilly isn't one of them!"

"No, not Dilly, but one or two of your other so-called buddies at the fire department," Bob answered.

"Who?"

"I'm sorry, Kate," he said gently, "we can't tell you that. In fact, we shouldn't be telling you this much, but we both felt that with everything you've been through you had a right to know."

I said nothing, feeling nauseous.

"We're building a good case against Abel Mertz," Bob added, squeezing my shoulder, "but again that's all I can tell you. Don't ask us anything more."

I sat in silence for a long time, chin in hand, staring out across the fields. Bob and Reverend Jessup sat quietly with me, allowing me to grieve and rage in silence. In the end, there was nothing else they or I could say. Bob gave me all the reassurance he could, saying he hoped to have Abel Mertz arrested before too long and that I'd be safe living at Donna and Neil's for the few days that remained until my departure. He also asked me to maintain secrecy about this because his ability to make further arrests hinged on his remaining undercover.

Both men held me close as we said good-bye. I was staggered by what they had revealed, staggered by the fact that some of the men I had worked with at the fire department for years saving lives, delivering babies, rescuing stranded hikers, had been living a lie. I comforted myself with the fact that I was now safe—I hoped—and that all I had to do was wrap up a few days of work for Hilary and take care of some personal things before I left Highton County for good.

If none of the resumes I'd sent out before my father got ill brought in a job offer, I'd just go home to my parents, and after that—well, I would cross that bridge when I came to it. A chapter of my life was closing, and maybe I should just be grateful I'd gotten out of it alive.

It's Usually the Least Likely Who Succeed

I was running late. I glanced again at my watch, hoping the minute hand might have reversed, but of course it hadn't. That's why I found myself alone in what should have been an overcrowded elevator in the Highton County Courthouse heading up to the presiding courtroom.

This would be my last hearing, and today was my last day as a North Carolina CPS social worker. But it wouldn't be my last day in this field. To my surprise, the California Department of Social and Health Services had offered me a position in their social work academy training program, and I had accepted it. In fact, I was looking forward to it. After nearly a decade of social service field work, I was burned out in more ways than one and ready to put field casework and everything about Highton County, North Carolina, far behind me.

I knew I wouldn't miss it. I would miss my friends and co-workers, and they had thrown me a great farewell party the night before. As a result I had overslept and was running late, and I knew the presiding judge would be more than a little miffed.

This was not a good note to end on. I sighed and leaned against the elevator wall and closed my eyes.

The elevator stopped on the second floor, and an attractive woman, perhaps thirty years old, stepped in. She was dressed in the usual spit-and-polish skirt, blazer, and heels of a paralegal and carried the requisite briefcase. Her hair was done up in a neat bun, and she was holding the hand of a beautiful girl of perhaps ten or eleven.

The elevator door slid shut, and we rode up toward "Presiding" in silence. The elevator stopped on the fourth floor, the floor that housed the offices of the public defenders.

The young woman pushed the "door open" button on the elevator to hold it in place and looked at me.

"You don't remember me, do you?" she said suddenly.

I started and studied her face. She was smiling. There was something vaguely familiar about her, but I couldn't place it. I shook my head. "I'm sorry, no, I don't."

"It's me—Marsha Braun."

For a moment the name did not register, and then my jaw dropped. Marsha Braun? My first client ever? My worst client ever? The woman I had despaired of, given up on, and was so happy to have off my case record? The woman who would never give up alcohol or drugs and probably never get her kids back?

My face must have registered my shock because she laughed. "Yes, it's me. I'm a paralegal for the PD's office. This is my youngest, Ellie. It's bring your daughter to work day." She squeezed Ellie's hand. "Say hi, Ellie. This lady used to be our social worker."

Ellie mumbled a quick "hi" then lowered her head.

Marsha returned her gaze to my face. "I've been clean and sober for almost six years. I'm in college and hoping to get into law school. My goal is to work here with CPS parents. I figured an attorney might be able to convince some of them that social workers are on their side."

She smiled again at her daughter. "My kids have been back with me for five years."

I was still too stunned to speak.

Marsha motioned for Ellie to step off the elevator and then held the door open with her hand. She turned to face me fully. "You know, you were the biggest pain in the ass I ever encountered. You never let up on me. You kept pushing, pushing, pushing to get me to clean up my act and pull my life together. I fought you tooth and toenail. God, how I hated you!" She paused and smiled. "Miss Kate, you were the best friend I ever had."

The elevator door slid shut. I cried all the way up to "Presiding."

Some Final Thoughts

I am told that life is a circle; that everything we do comes around again and again, until we learn our lessons and make the right choices. Our mistakes and weaknesses become our greatest teachers; our failures give us a chance to grow. If I learned anything from my decade in the field, it is this: that the human spirit is unquenchable; that given a chance, even the least among us can grow to stand among the greatest. Everything we do in life is like tossing a pebble into a still pond—our actions ripple out and affect others, often in ways we cannot anticipate or even understand.

I sometimes think back to what Maryann Tevis taught me: to try and see the dignity and beauty beneath filthy clothing and unwashed skin; to see the pride in owning a home even if it's a trailer and has no running water, heat, or insulation. I think about how a few parenting classes and the simple act of placing a somewhat misshapen bouquet of flowers on a filthy table in a filthy kitchen could ripple into changing a life.

I learned that Maryann was right and that the greatest successes often come from the most hopeless and least likely places. And while she had once lectured me that food, shelter, and clothing were essentials to survival, she had insisted that they were secondary to what I now know matters most: kindness, love, respect, but most of all, dignity.

– Kathryn Anne Michaels

Breaking the Cycle of Abuse

The first step in preventing the sexual abuse of children is to accept that it exists. The next step is to be brave enough to believe the child and intervene.

The "typical" child victim:

- can be either a boy or a girl and, in most cases, knows and trusts the abuser
- can be an infant, toddler, preschooler, or school-aged child up to age eighteen
- comes from any socioeconomic background, ethnic, or religious group
- is usually afraid to tell anyone about the sexual abuse for fear of being blamed or punished
- is rarely abused by a stranger

Who sexually abuses children?

Anyone can. Child abusers can be immediate or extended family members (fathers, mothers, stepparents, grandparents, siblings, uncles, aunts, cousins, etc.). They can be neighbors, babysitters, religious leaders, teachers, coaches, or anyone else who has close contact with a child.

These warning signs could suggest that someone is sexually abusing a child. While not indicative of abuse, these behaviors can be considered cause for concern:

1. Making others uncomfortable by ignoring social, emotional, or physical boundaries or limits.
2. Refusing to let a child set his or her own limits. Using teasing or belittling language to keep a child from setting a limit.
3. Insisting on hugging, touching, kissing, tickling, wrestling with, or holding a child even when the child does not want this physical contact or attention.
4. Turning to a child for emotional or physical comfort by sharing personal or private information or activities that are normally shared with other adults.
5. Frequently pointing out sexual images or telling inappropriate or suggestive jokes with children present.
6. Exposing a child to adult sexual interactions without apparent concern.
7. Having secret interactions with teens or children (e.g., playing adult games or sharing drugs, alcohol, or sexual material) or spending excessive time e-mailing, text-messaging, or calling children or youths.
8. Being overly interested in the sexuality of a certain child or teen (e.g., talks repeatedly about the child's developing body or interferes with normal teen dating).
9. Insisting on or managing to spend unusual amounts of uninterrupted time alone with a child.
10. Seems "too good to be true" (e.g., frequently babysits different children for free, takes them on special outings alone, buys them gifts or gives them money for no apparent reason).
11. Frequently walks in on children/teens in the bathroom.

12. Allows children or teens to consistently get away with inappropriate behaviors.

How can you help?

1. Become a foster parent.
2. Consider adoption, especially of older, difficult to place children.
3. Volunteer in organizations that provide support or shelter to disadvantaged or troubled youth.
4. Contact your local Child Protective Services office and ask what you can do to help.
5. Become a Big Brother or Big Sister volunteer.

28367913R00122

Made in the USA
Lexington, KY
14 January 2019